Abdulmotaleb El Saddik

Interactive Multimedia Learning

Shared Reusable Visualization-based Modules

With 60 Figures and 16 Tables

 Springer

Abdulmotaleb El Saddik
Darmstadt University of Technology
Department of Electrical Engineering
and Information Technology KOM
Merckstraße 25
64283 Darmstadt
Germany

Library of Congress Cataloging-in-Publication Data
El Saddik, Abdulmotaleb, 1966-
    Interactive multimedia learning: shared reusable visualization-based modules/
    Abdulmotaleb El Saddik.
        p.cm.
    Includes bibliographical references and index.
    ISBN 3540419306 (pbk.: alk. Paper)
    1. Interactive multimedia. 2. Computer-assisted instruction. 3. Multimedia systems.
    4. Instructional systems–Design. I. Title.

    LB1028.55 .E42 2001
    371.33'4–dc21   2001042863

ISBN 3-540-41930-6 Springer-Verlag Berlin Heidelberg New York

Springer-Verlag Berlin Heidelberg New York
a member of BertelsmannSpringer Science+Business Media GmbH
http://www.springer.de

© Springer-Verlag Berlin Heidelberg 2001
Printed in Germany

Cover design: KünkelLopka, Heidelberg
Typesetting: Camera-ready by the author
Printed on acid-free paper   SPIN: 10835520   33/3142 GF– 5 4 3 2 1 0

University of Hertfordshire

Learning and Information Services

Hatfield Campus Learning Resources Centre
College Lane Hatfield Herts AL10 9AB
Renewals: Tel 01707 284673 Mon-Fri 12 noon-8pm only

This book is in heavy demand and is due back strictly by the last date stamped below. A fine will be charged for the late return of items.

ONE WEEK LOAN

Springer

Berlin
Heidelberg
New York
Barcelona
Hong Kong
London
Milan
Paris
Tokyo

O Lord, Enhance my Knowledge
— Holy Quoran

Abstract

Educational software has been developed with the potential for online learning. Some examples are complete packages, commercially prepared and disseminated. Many, however, are individual programs, which often represent excellent applications of sophisticated computing capabilities and a good contribution to the library of educational software. However, they lack cohesion as an organized collection because every software application is vertically engineered to comply within its specific domain. This makes reuse and sharing more difficult, and can lead to maintenance and deployment difficulties as restrictive platform requirements accumulate over time.

Multibook is a web-based adaptive hypermedia learning system for multimedia and communication technology. It focuses on providing end-users with specific lessons tailored to a targeted group. These lessons are created using a knowledge base of multimedia elements, especially interactive animations.

In this work, several concepts with respect to the development and reusability of multimedia content in web-based learning systems are introduced. More particularly, the development of a component-based framework, which enables developers to employ reusable software components enhanced with metadata, creates complete instructional visualizations for a given subject and integrates these visualizations in an appropriate learning context.

Moreover, in this work two activities for making stand-alone visualizations group-aware are addressed: transparent sharing of the same instructional visualization with diverse views in a moderated session, and organization of interactions in the shared workspace. No other work has addressed the issue of transparent collaboration, based on instructional visualizations enhanced with metadata in such a way.

Proof of concept is provided by the implementation of the component-based framework "iTBeanKit", and the integration of the developed instructional visualizations in the Multibook prototype, as well as in the shared environment "JASMINE", developed also during this work. JASMINE is an extension of Multibook to support group work. Experiments are conducted to show how reusing the same visualization in different learning contexts can be achieved.

There is power in forgiveness

For my parents, Hamdi and Ikram

Acknowledgments

I am particularly grateful for the continuous support, motivation, and guidance of my teacher and supervisor Prof. Dr.-Ing. Ralf Steinmetz during my work and research at KOM. Without his help none of this would have been possible. He has constantly been available with great ideas and suggestions, providing me with more than the needed facilities. He has been an exemplary guide and mentor.

Furthermore, I would like to thank Prof. Dr. Nicolas Georganas. He has been extremely supportive of this endeavor and willing to provide wise and constructive feedback during my visit to MCRLab, at the University of Ottawa.

I would also like to thank Dr. Carsten Griwodz for the diverse discussions. Carsten was always a discussion partner, even if we sometimes had different opinions. He was always there to give me feedback. I took up a lot of his time, discussing my endeavor.

Special thanks to my colleagues in the multimedia communications group (KOM), especially Dr. Stephan Fischer who helped me clarify a lot of ideas. I am both grateful and indebted for their support of my efforts.

Additionally, I would like to thank Amir Ghavam for the valuable discussions about component software. Special thanks goes to Ziad Sakr and Vasilios Darlagiannis for being great friends and even under extreme time pressure, being ready to proof read this work, providing me with suggestions and help.

Finally, I am most grateful to my wife, Ligia, my two daughters Ikram and Yasmin, my sisters, and my brother for their continued support. During the last four years, I did not offer them the time they deserved, but still, they have continued to be my closest friends, providing love and commitment always.

Table of Contents

x   ▪   Table of Contents
       ▪
       ▪

List of Figures

List of Tables

Chapter 1 Introduction

1.1 Motivation

The primary motivation for using multimedia technologies in education is the belief that they will support superior forms of learning. Advances in cognitive psychology have inculcated our understanding of the nature of skilled intellectual performance and provided a basis for designing environments wholesome to learning. There is now a widespread agreement among teachers, educators, and psychologists [CBN89] that advanced skills of comprehension, reasoning, composition, and experimentation are acquired not only by the "transmission" of facts but also by the learner's interaction with content, which caught teachers' attention first. Albert Bork, professor of Physics at the University of California at Irvine and strong computer interaction advocate, described interactive learning as "the most valuable aspect of the computer in education...with students constantly cast as participants in the process rather than spectators" [Tay80]. His work concentrated on the use of primitive computer graphics to visualize Physics concepts, but he also emphasized that "there is not a single way, but a whole variety of ways" [Tay80] in which to use computers for teaching.

Furthermore, computing is now more available and affordable than ever before. Conventional as well as mobile networks help in transmitting instructional material to sites thousands of kilometers away. Diverse computer applications make it possible not only for university students, but also for school children to do a lot of things, from building their own curriculum materials in hypermedia formats to communicating with their counterparts on the other side of the world to collecting and analyzing data much as practicing scientists would. While the most sophisticated technology remains in the hands of the few, it is becoming more and more affordable and available. At the same time, use of educationally sophisticated material is provided in commonplace technologies, such as videotape, CD, DVD, and the World Wide Web.

Moreover, the rapid advancement in multimedia technology [SN95] generates new forms of media and communications, which can be used to increase the quality of educational materials. The diverse compression techniques [ES98], [MPFL97], such as JPEG,

MPEG1, MPEG2 and MPEG4 as well as visualizations and animations can be seen as examples of such media. At the same time video conferencing systems [Wil00], the multicast communication protocol [Fdi96] and the Resource Reservation Protocol [BZB⁺97] are examples of the development of the network and communication technology [Tan96].

Yet, new forms of multimedia communication technology will not educate students without the strong need for high quality content. To help students learn difficult concepts, interactive learning software needs specific capabilities for simulation, visualization, and tools for analyzing, modeling, and annotating data. Such interactive, dynamic representations are the core content of educational learning modules. These representations have to be combined flexibly with many kinds of contexts: diverse classroom presentations, tutorials, experimentation notebooks and tests [PED⁺99] and [EFS00].

Often, instructional software does not get used because the available software is simply irrelevant to the instructor's curricular goals. Most of the more sophisticated, inventive pieces of instructional software deal with only a narrow slice of curriculum or with material that is fairly trivial in itself. At the same time, instructors report intense pressure to "cover" an unrealistically large amount of required material.

Instructional software today is locally effective, but globally fragmentary. Hence, to date, it has had limited impact in systematic curricular reforms, and is failing to meet large scale needs for re-use of interactive content. For example, it is awkward to combine interactive visualization modules that are each valuable in their own niche, and theoretically complementary in ensemble. The user, for example, cannot connect an animation of a video decoder to that of a network and study the resulting effects [ESS⁺99].

Ongoing research in the area of instructional visualizations sheds insight into factors that contribute to the design of effective visualization systems [HNS98], and suggests that attempts over the last two decades at using visualizations to teach algorithm behavior were unsatisfactory, not because of a flaw with animation and visualization as a technique, but perhaps due to the approach used to convey the animations.

Today there are several standards efforts specifically targeted at advanced educational technologies [ARI00], [Gro00] and [IMS00], repositories for educational object components have been built [Eoe00] and [GEM00]. These efforts gain leverage from the rise of interactive Web technology and its associated emphasis on standards-based interoperability. Emerging solutions for component-based systems include development frameworks (JavaBeans [ON98'] and ActiveX [Dav96]), shared communication protocols RMI and CORBA [OH98], markup languages HTML and XML [Hol00], and metadata formats [DC00], [Gro00] and [IMS00].

One of the key problems in developing educational software systems in general and interactive instructional visualization units in particular is planning for change. Educational systems must be flexible in that they must be easy to adapt to new and changing user requirements. The state of the art way of dealing with open requirements is to build systems out of reusable components conforming to a plug-in architecture [KBKT99], [EFS00]. The functionality of such systems can then be changed or extended by substituting or plugging in new components. Although the component-based solutions developed to date are useful [KH98], [BRM98] they are inadequate for those building component-based interactive learning environments in which the components must respond to the meaning of the content as well as its form and presentation.

Recapitulating the above, it is obvious that the development and description of interactive instructional visualization units and the integration of these modules in web-based learning systems according to user preferences and knowledge in the "appropriate context" is a problem. As a consequence, not surprisingly, a number of issues arise. Among others are the level of granularity of the developed visualizations, the application of adequate metadata to describe them and the issue of sharing the same phenomena with diverse views in a managed collaborative session. The above-mentioned issues are not separately addressed, but rather treated as parts of a framework, which has been developed and tested within the Multibook project [Mul00].

1.2 Requirements

To present the requirements, which need to be addressed by the framework presented in this work, a usage scenario will be used consisting of a set of "situations" in using instructional visualizations. Since the desired framework is intended for educational use, three roles can be identified: the developer, who is in charge of creating the content or writing the appropriate code of the topic to be visualized, the educator, who becomes the designer of the visualization, and the learner, who becomes the end-user of the animated phenomena. It should be noted that a user can have more than one role at a time. A teacher for instance can be both the content creator and the content developer. It can be stated that:

> "Learning becomes more and more multimedia and cooperative, learning requires mobility, modularization & cooperation"
>
> *Dagstuhl Seminar 2000 "Multimedia for Multimedia:*
> *Learning and Teaching in the Next Decade"*
> — Ralf Steinmetz

Usage Scenario

An educator (teacher) uses the Internet to deploy a collaboration session providing the users (students) located in several distributed locations with the ability to take part on his lecture. Using the environment, teacher and students can conduct their activities, closely collaborating on topic explained within the course. Some elements of this lecture are visualization-based, illustrating the behavior of some phenomena or topics. As a matter of fact, the teacher wants to use the same instructional unit in both his face-to-face as well as on-line (both synchronous and asynchronous) lecture. Thus collaboration facilities are needed, which make use of the multimedia elements in the lecture in a transparent way and therefore reuse already developed stand-alone applications collaboratively.

Sometimes, for instance, in a test situation, the teacher wants to see more information on his graphical user interface than his students, without the need to re-write any new applications. He wants to adjust both, the level of explanation and the level of interactivity of an animation, thus influencing the presentation and the results of the topic being illustrated according to a desired level of functionality and appearance, suitable for the specific needs of the students.

Since students maybe distributed in different locations, it is possible that they are using different platforms. Some of them may be equipped with PCs, while others with SUN workstations or Mac systems. Nevertheless they should be able to communicate and take part in the lecture.

To use interactive visualizations in the lecture, multimedia elements should be developed. The development of multimedia content in general and instructional visualizations in particular is costly and time-consuming [GG95]. Thus, reusing the same building blocks (raw content like video or code) for several applications is important, since the new applications will require less time for their development and will cost much less than developing their content totally from scratch.

The user interface of the current educational visualization system remains the medium to which the end-user (student) interacts with. Thus the developed instructional visualizations should be intuitive to use. Students do not have to care about the graphical presentation, but concentrate on the visualized topic. As a consequence following requirements arise:

• Requirement 1: Reuse of building blocks.
• Requirement 2: Changing user requirements and knowledge should be considered.
• Requirement 3: Interoperability and platform independency.
• Requirement 4: Usability of instructional visualization.
• Requirement 5: Reuse stand-alone applications in a shared environment.
• Requirement 6: Support the sharing of the same visualization with different views.

This work focuses specifically on gains that can be achieved by reducing development and use efforts by reusing or sharing work. The approach taken here will be addressed next.

1.3 Research Approach

To gain an insight into the state of the art in this research direction and to consider how much of the above listed requirements have been considered, a survey of instructional visualization systems was the start of this work. The results are discussed in Chapter 2.

Two distinct situations to reuse information have been considered to accomplish the reusability requirement (req. #1). The first situation is the reuse of code from existing applications or code repositories to build new applications. Software engineering aspects with respect to developing reusable learning units have been discussed, and compared with each other aiming to find an appropriate way to use in the development process.

The second situation to reuse information is the case when, within the same application, or within different applications the same objects (not necessary code) are reused. Different solutions to describe, find, use and reuse instructional information can be found in the literature. All of them deal with static data. Instructional visualizations, however, are multimedia elements with dynamic content, that is why work in this book has been made to investigate the possibility to describe dynamic multimedia content in order to find, use and reuse them.

To describe such interactive visualizations, a new set of metadata is introduced, which is an extension of the IEEE's Learning Objects Metadata (LOM). Component software revealed in this work can be used in combination with metadata in order to address changing user requirement and knowledge (req. #2). The use and re-use visualization learning artifacts in different learn context will be discussed in Chapter 4.

To perform the usability requirement (req. #4), one should study the impact of the graphical user interface and how the diverse graphical elements should be distributed on the GUI of the visualization. The best form to present data should also be investigated. It was out of the scope of my research to investigate a new way for presenting multimedia content. In this work, results from the human computer interaction (HCI) research community has been taken and integrated in the developed framework. Nevertheless usability studies have been conducted on the developed framework in order to prove that the proposed technique is suitable and useful.

Interoperability is a huge research area and was out of the scope of this work. The platform independency requirement (req. #3) was not considered as a research question. However, interoperability and platform independency was taken into consideration during the implementation part of this work as discussed in Chapters 4 and 5.

As a consequence to the first 4 requirements (req. #1, 2, 3 and 4) a component-based framework enhanced with dynamic metadata for the development of instructional visualization has been developed. This framework has been integrated into a web-based learning system, the Multibook. Experiments have been conducted to prove how reusing the same visualization in different context affects the usability (Chapter 4).

Multibook, does not consider group work, and so the shared use of visualizations is made clumsy and difficult. To comply with requirements (req. #5) and (req. #6), techniques for making visualizations group-aware resources was investigated. In particular, this work has looked at two activities to sharing interactive visualizations: transparent sharing of the same visualization with diverse views, and organization of interactions in the shared space. A transparent collaborative tool is also presented in this work along with performance evaluation (Chapter 5).

1.4 Contributions

The major contributions of this work are summarized as follows:

- The design of a component-based framework, which separates the development process of instructional visualizations from the integration process in an appropriate context.
- A novel way of using metadata, as parameter that can be passed to multimedia content in order to change the behaviour of the content and therefore to tailor multimedia elements according to user needs.
- A new metadata classification scheme that considers metadata for dynamic content as well as metadata for static content.
- The design of a mechanism which allows transparent collaboration. This mechanism is more efficient than the existing ones. It replicates collaboration un-aware applications on each client and multicast the events.

- A novel approach that considers sharing of different views of the same application in a moderated collaborative environment.

As a direct result of this research, several journal papers and conference papers have been published. They are listed among my other publications at the end of this book. Furthermore, twenty Study and Diploma (Studien und Diplomarbeit) theses have been supervised. In addition a number of interactive instructional applets, visualizing different multimedia and communication network protocols and algorithms, have been developed. Some of them can be found on the enclosed CD.

1.5 Outline

In the following, the outline of the work is given:

Chapter 2 gives an overview of interactive visualization learning systems and reviews related work in instructional visualization systems.

Chapter 3 discusses the re-usability issues of interactive visualization units in learning systems. This issue is twofold: a) Content creation, in which the design and development of interactive visualization learning modules is considered and b) Re-usability of the content through the use of metadata, which must be considered during the tagging, and the integration process of the visualization within an appropriate context.

Chapter 4 addresses the Multibook system and gives an explanation about its architecture and usage. It shows how a component-based framework for the development of interactive instructional visualizations enhanced with metadata are integrated within the Multibook. This Chapter ends with a user evaluation.

Chapter 5 answers the collaboration question through the description of the transparent collaborative tool JASMINE.

Chapter 6 concludes this work and gives an outlook of future work.

Chapter 2 Visualization and Animation in Education

Authors, teachers, and tutors tried to explain and visualize abstract concepts and complex ideas by means other than the printed word. While at the beginning pictures were used, nowadays the computer provides more sophisticated ways to visualize data, ideas, concepts, facts, and algorithms. The ancient Chinese proverb:

Tell me and I forget
Show me and I remember
Involve me and I understand

still holds true in the multimedia age. Scientific visualization, mathematical visualization, program visualization, and algorithm animation are well-known concepts in the academic community.

This Chapter presents an overview of visualization in the electrical and computer science field. It is broken down in the following fashion. First, definition of instructional visualization is given. The motivation for using visualization and visual techniques in instruction is presented, followed by a discussion of when the use of visualization is most appropriate. The broad spectrum of uses of visualization in education is then considered. This spectrum is organized from static to dynamic and from passive to active in terms of students' involvement with the visualization artifact. Types of visualizations are then categorized, followed by a survey of visualization systems depicting the state of the art in this research area.

2.1 Computer-based Visualization: Definitions and Goals

The idea to benefit from visualization in the context of education was first exploited in the 1960s starting extensive developments. Since the focus of this study is visualization and animation in education, first some common definitions of visualization in general need to be introduced.

Informally, visualization is the transformation of information or data into pictures. In science often large and/or complex collections of data have to be processed. Usually it is not suitable for human beings (students, researchers, etc...) to investigate such data-sets by reading lists of numbers or other textual representations. The mapping of information into graphs or images, i.e., visualization, was already identified as a powerful tool for data investigation a long time ago. Several definitions of the term "visualization" can be found in relevant dictionaries and respective literature, e. g.:

- Visualization means to make visual or visible, to form a mental image of, to make perceptible to the mind or imagination [IPOLD00].
- The act of making a visible presentation of numerical data, particularly a graphical one. This might include anything from a simple X-Y graph of one dependent variable against one independent variable to a virtual reality world which allows you to fly around the data [oC00].
- Using the computer to convert data into picture form. The most basic visualization is that of turning transaction data and summary information into charts and graphs [tedoctc00].

Visualization tools can be used in a variety of teaching situations: a picture or an interactive animation, self-learning or in classroom demonstrations, open or closed laboratories, and traditional assignments. The student can be a passive viewer of information or an active participant in the visualization process, and involved in instructor-led, individual, or collaborative work. In the following some motivating factors for instructional use of visualization tools are presented [Nap96] and [Glo97]:

- *Individual improvement of students' understanding*:
  Using an interactive visualization, students can playfully and without stress explore the peculiarities of an algorithm. By allowing students to manipulate algorithms and their input, and then study the resulting actions of the algorithm, they are able to form a conceptual model of the algorithm in addition to learning the code. They also can modify parameters and analyze algorithms empirically.
- *Skill mastery through additional practice opportunities*:
  Students get a new way to experience algorithms. In addition to doing paper exercises and writing programs, they can perceive algorithms visually and study their features by watching and interacting with animations. It presents somehow safe experience, because data can be lost without damage, i.e., in chemical interactive visualization.
- *Development of analytic skills*:
  Visualizations assist in the development of analytic skills, as students are asked to collect their own experiences for algorithm analysis and subsequent design of improved algorithms.
- *Motivation enhancement*:
  Through appealing presentation of the complex material, students are better motivated to study complicated subjects. Because it is private, students "ask" whatever they want; no one will laugh, no one will scold.

- *Presentation aid in the classroom*:

  Visualizations support the teacher in explaining the dynamic behavior of an algorithm during the lecture. If computer screen projection is available in the classroom, the teacher can run instructional visualizations interactively to compare, for example, the search/found ratio of diverse disk scheduling algorithms [Ste00] using the same data input.

In the following, the use of visualization in education will be investigated with more details.

2.2 Instructional Use of Visualizations

Instructional visualization has its roots in educational film and in mathematical visualization. It has also been influenced by recent developments in scientific data visualization, which is at present an extremely diverse and active field. Algorithm animation visualizes the activity of an algorithm through moving images. As in conventional animation, the movement of images is not real, but is simulated by presenting the viewer with a sequence of still images. Unlike conventional animation, however, in instructional visualization the sequence of images is not fixed. Each image represents the state of the algorithm at some point in time. Since the inputs to an algorithm can vary, its behavior will vary and hence so will the animation of that behavior.

Several different approaches exist to classify instructional visualizations. One possible way draws a graph with the root being scientific visualization and letting all other types be branches of it. For example software visualization is dealt with as a branch of scientific visualization, which is concerned with visualizing software objects including algorithms, programs and parallel processes. Many visualization techniques have moved beyond the scientific domain and into areas of business, social science, demographics, and information management in general.

2.2.1 Scientific and Engineering Visualization

Scientific and engineering visualization uses the computer to display real-world objects that cannot normally be seen, such as the shapes of molecules, air and fluid dynamics and weather patterns. Many times scientific visualization requires enormous computing resources, and the supercomputer centers and national laboratories throughout the world are always at the forefront of such activity [RER98].

The area of Scientific and Engineering Visualization is sometimes extended to include the term Industrial Visualization. Scientific visualization is distinct from other visualization in that it deals solely with the scientific data. Due to large volumes of data typically gained through observations, remote sensing and measuring, users are most often only able to view and understand a small fraction of data at a time. Scientific visualization attempts to convert this deluge of data into color images (or, sometimes, sounds), in order to convey the information produced to the user in a manner that can be easily assimilated [HDP92] and [HPS+94].

Typical applications are rendering satellite data, numerical simulation, tomography, meteo-rology, climatology, geology and oceanography, involving research fields like astronomy, physics, chemistry, molecular biology, meteorology, geosciences, anthropology, space exploration, aviation, medicine, architecture or industrial design.

2.2.2 Mathematical Visualization

Although the area of Mathematics can be seen as part of the Sciences, mathematical visual-ization is itself a very vast and extensive field and is therefore presented apart from scientific and engineering visualization described above. The realm of mathematical visualization is far-reaching and a lot of research has been done in this area alone with many ideas forming the basis of further developments [Hep00].

Mathematical Visualization offers efficient visualization tools to the classical subjects of mathematics, and applies mathematical techniques to problems in computer graphics and scientific visualization. Originally, it started in the interdisciplinary area of differential geometry, numerical mathematics, and computer graphics. In recent years, the methods developed have found other important applications [HP98] [Pal]. Mathematical visualiza-tion is also described as the art of creating tangible experiences with abstract mathematical objects and their transformations.

2.2.3 Information Visualization

The term "Information Visualization" commonly stands for representing data in 3-D images in order to navigate through it more quickly and access it in a more natural manner. Origi-nally the term was coined at Xerox's Palo Alto Research Center, which has developed very advanced techniques. Multidimensional cubes or pivot tables are simple forms of informa-tion visualization that are widely used today [Shn97].

The impact of this area of research is that it deals with developing ways of visualizing information sources and data as means towards helping people interpret and understand such information. In particular, focus is put on depicting large information spaces, which often contain more informational elements than there are pixels on the screen. The origins of this work direction are visualizations of large programs and software systems [Shn96], [NS99], and [PS95].

2.2.4 Computation Visualization

Price, Backer and Small [PSS93] define software visualization as the use of crafts of typo-graphy, graphics design, animation, and cinematography with modern human-computer interaction and computer graphics technology to facilitate both the human understanding and effective use of computer software [Boy97]. Visualization of Computation (synonymous Software Visualization) can be divided into [PSS93]:

- *Program Visualization*:
  Program visualization consists of producing views of program executions that can be textual or, e.g., animated. It is not limited to algorithms or activities that are evident in

the source-code for the program. They may include activity in the compiled code, the run-time system, data, and even the underlying hardware. Most program visualization systems are confined to one programming language, which usually is the same as the language used to write the visualization system. There exist several uses of program visualization, among other are the following:

- Teaching
- Debugging
- Evaluating and improving program performance
- Evaluating and reducing resource utilization
- Evaluation of algorithms in the context of complete programs and real data
- Understanding program behavior

- *Algorithm Animation* (algorithm visualization)

  Algorithm animation creates an abstraction of both the data structure and the behavior of an algorithm. This can be done by mapping the current values of the parameters used in the algorithm into an image, which then gets animated based on the operations between two succeeding states in the execution of the algorithm [Glo97].

  Besides the developments concerning animation in the motion picture industry, the advent of computer graphics technology in the late 1970s and early 1980s brought with it new opportunities to illustrate algorithms. Illustrations moved from paper to computer screen, as computer scientists developed the first computer systems to facilitate the creation of so-called algorithm animations, animated illustrations of algorithms in action. Due to the limits of the technology of the time, the first systems could do little more than aid in the production of algorithm movies. With the help of that system, "Sorting Out Sorting" [Boy97], a legendary instructional film on sorting algorithms was produced. By taking advantage of emerging graphical workstation technology, later systems supported interactive environments for exploring algorithm pictures and animations [Bro88a], [Sta90b], [Sta93], [Bro91], [HM98], [HNS98], [KBKT99] and [SSvD99].

  Three areas where algorithm animation has traditionally been used are:

  - Teaching
  - Evaluating Algorithms
  - Improving Algorithms

This distinction is based upon the level of abstraction of the two visualization approaches. Program Visualization is concerned with making apparent low-level implementation details of programs such as code structure and data types. Algorithm visualization deals with the more abstract problem of describing how an algorithm works. Whereas program visualizations should explicate specific implementation details, algorithm visualizations can be suggestive of a variety of coding strategies.

Visual programming is often described together with software visualization, but it is a concept quite different. While in visualization the program is specified in a textually manner and the image is employed to illustrate its aspects, the visual programming involves the use of graphical images to create the program itself. A number of visual programming tools exist. These tools are usually integrated in IDE (Integrated Development Environments),

Examples of such tools are: Microsoft Visual series (C, Basic, Java), Borland Jbuilder, IBM Visual Age series (C, C++, Java) and Symantec Visual Café.

2.3 Spectrum of Instructional Visualization Systems

In the classroom, instructional visualizations are often employed in the demonstration of a topic. Given the power of a visualization to illustrate abstractions, visualization tools may be appropriately used before, after and during the discussion of a topic. Before, because of the ability of visualizations to abstract from implementation details, and after, to reinforce lecture material such as algorithm details. It is thus important that a visualization tool allows access to the topic under investigation from different viewpoints and at multiple levels of abstraction. This will be investigated in more detail in Chapter 4.

Depending on the learn context, on the user level and on the topic itself, all forms of visualization, ranging from the simplest form of a picture to the more complex form of an interactive simulation, can be used in the teaching of Engineering and Computer Science concepts and algorithms, as well as in the medical and natural sciences fields.

A visualization in the form of a picture is used when the amount of data is small, the data structure is very simple, or when the relationship of objects is important, but movement is not needed. When the data structure is very simple, a picture of the data structure is much clearer than a textual description of it ("A picture is worth a thousand words"). For example, a picture of a power plant is much clearer to understand than a textual description of each element of the plant and a description of how elements are connected together. Furthermore, the description of a full tank can be easily illustrated with two pictures, the initial empty tank and the final full tank with an arrow showing the direction of the valve to open.

A visualization in the form of an interactive animation is used when the quantity of data is large, the data structure is complex, or when movement is needed to show the relationships between objects change over time. When a large quantity of data is used, an animation can show how this data is processed. For example, the illustration of the shellsort algorithm must use a large amount of data in order to show several partition breakdowns. As another example, illustrating the binary search algorithm and its analysis is more effective using a large amount of data to show how fast one can find a particular element. When a data structure is complex and/or changes of the data structure are to be discussed, an animation can show these complexities and movements much more easily than one could show them on a blackboard.

Seeing pictures is often not enough to understand the phenomena behind the presented data. Interactivity is therefore necessary. It implies 'doing' as opposed to 'being', action and reaction with another whether it is a computer, a person, or the surrounding environment. In a non-interactive lecture the lecturer will talk and the students will listen. In an interactive lecture the lecturer invites questions and comments from the students and a discussion ensues. In an everyday sense when you drive you are responding interactively with the surrounding environment and traffic. Interaction is an accepted part of our everyday life. Interactivity in learning is a necessary and fundamental mechanism for knowledge acquisition and the development of both cognitive and physical skills. Regarding the algorithm visualization system's characteristics as a teaching tool, not primarily tapering towards automation, puts the focus on its advanced interactive capabilities [Sim99] which will be discussed in further details in Section 2.3.2.

Besides the level of interactivity an animation system provides, there are several factors by which the educative potential of algorithm animation systems can be measured. Certainly of chief importance is the level of abstraction afforded by the system. The abstraction must provide enough detail to explicate the process while abstracting pragmatic trivialities that may obscure the process. The best abstraction level provides the quickest mental path to the semantics of the topic to be explained [SFC94]

Abstraction of information into visual forms plays a key role in the development of algorithm animations. A classification for abstraction as applied to algorithm animation will be outlined in the following. The classification emphasizes the expressive power of the abstraction, ranging from simple direct presentation of the program's state to complex animations intended to explain the behavior of a program.

2.3.1 Degree of Abstraction

Fundamentally, visualization exploits the extraordinarily high speed with which humans are able do detect and track visual patterns to compactly transmit information. Many ways exist in which visual information can be used to represent data. Shape, size, color, texture, and arrangement of objects are only a few of the attributes which provide a rich visual vocabulary. However, the very richness of this vocabulary means that care must be used in selecting and presenting information to the viewer [Bro88b]. In the following each of the representations [CR92] will be explained in more detail:

- *Direct representation*:
  stands for the most primitive graphical representations, which are obtained by mapping some aspect of the program directly to a picture. Because only very limited abstraction mechanisms are employed, it is often the case that the original information can be easily reconstructed from the graphical representation. Such a mapping may loosely be considered as a bijection between some appropriate subset of the state and the image.

- *Structural representation:*
  is considered to be more abstract representation, that may be obtained by concealing or encapsulating some of the details associated with the program and using a direct representation of the remaining information. The goal is to exhibit the inherent structure of the information that is visualized. Some information is lost, but the overall presentation may be enhanced through the elimination of extraneous details. A typical application of structural abstraction would be in a visualization of a computation running on a network of processes, where the states of the individual processes might be reduced to a simple "active" or "inactive".

- *Synthesized representation*:
  is used to refer to an abstraction in which the information of interest is not directly represented in the program but can be derived from the program data. This shift of perspective often occurs when the data representations selected by the programmer come into con-

flict with the needs of the animator, particularly where the animator is attempting to extract and present some of the more abstract concepts of the algorithm which have no explicit representation in the program. The animator must then construct and maintain a representation that is more convenient for his particular needs.

- *Analytical representation*:
  attempts to capture abstract program properties, such as those used in correctness proofs. The goal of such abstractions is to de-emphasize the operational mechanics of program execution and focus on issues that are important in analytical thinking about the program. The approach is rooted in the notion that properties that are important in reasoning formally about programs should, when translated into visual form, also help the viewer understand the program's behavior.

- *Explanatory representation*:
  belongs to the field of sophisticated visualizations, that go beyond presenting simple representations of, e. g., a program state and use a variety of visual techniques to illustrate program behavior. These visual events often have no counterparts in the computation being depicted by the animation. They are added to improve the educative quality of the presentation, out of the desire to communicate the implications of a particular computational event, and in order to focus the viewer's attention. In essence, the animator takes the liberty of adding events to the representation of the program in order to "tell the story" better.

These levels of abstraction are listed in increasing order of abstractive power, although in practice the distinctions between the levels are fuzzy and many visualizations mix several techniques. Explanatory presentations in particular have a wide range of expressive power, in that the basic technique (the use of visual events to guide the viewer's understanding) can be applied to most visualizations.

2.3.2 Degree of Interactivity

When using visualizations in the delivery of educational content, different levels of interactivity can be distinguished. The idea of actively engaging the user with the learning object has its roots in the diverse learning theories [KfFK96], [And96] and [Kos96] with the degree of engagement varying according to the theory's principles, which are outlined in the following:

- *Behaviorism*:
  The behaviorist movement dates back to around 1920, slowing down around 1990, mainly stressing the idea that learning itself means stressing associations and composing simple associations into more complex skills. The design of learning environments consequently tries to support routines of activity so learning is efficient. Clear goals and immediate feedback are also desired features. Individualization with technology is considered to be useful [KfFK96].

- *Cognitivism*:
  Cognitivism arose in the 1960's. Learning in this context is seen to be the individual's own active discovery of concepts, theories, strategies and structures. The design of learn-

ing environments has to follow this idea by enabling individuals to engage in the interactive construction of their understanding through exploration, experimentation and problem solving [And96].

- *Constructivism*:
  Constructivism has been around since 1990. Learning is considered to be the process of becoming a member of a community, and becoming attuned to affordances as well as to actions that the environment provides [Kos96]. Knowledge is constructed in complex and real situations by the learner.

Behaviorist is sometimes called empiricist, cognitive can be found as rational and the constructive way has been called the situated or pragmatist approach. Many more philosophical and pedagogical combinations emphasizing certain aspects of the branches exist but they are out of the scope of this work and therefore will be not further discussed.

As mentioned above the degree of interactivity varies not only according to the system's general conception, but also within certain environments, according to the particular pedagogical paradigms. A common fragmentation looks at basically three steps [Glo98]:

- Viewing / Observing Mode:
  In the viewing / observing mode, the algorithm follows a given chronological order. The viewer is expected to plainly view and observe the steps of an algorithm in a visual presentation. There is no intention to have the viewer predict certain steps or develop part of the algorithm. Such view-only systems demonstrate one or more concepts with no interactive control. Moreover, these demonstrations are often considered useful when first introducing a concept or an algorithm. An example would be much like watching a video, where the viewer has no control over the presentation. The instructional surroundings delivers the educational context for the visualization, not the object itself.
- Tracing / Keeping Track Mode:
  In the tracing / keeping track mode, the user is supposed to predict the next step of the algorithm repeatedly. There is only one "correct" next step, the one the standard algorithm would do next. For this purpose, the learner interacts with the visualization of the data structure using the graphical user interface. The possibilities of a graphical user interface (GUI) are to be used for interaction when possible and useful, like pointing directly at data objects in the graphics of the visualization (e. g., using mouse clicks). One step of an algorithm often consists of the call of a function.
- Experimenting Mode:
  The third step called the experimenting mode is supposed to offer "discovering" of the algorithm. The topic to be learned is not presented as a completed work to the learner, but part of the development and discovery work should be repeated, enabling the learner to explore the visualization. This mode, offering the highest level of interactivity, moves from learning about prepared algorithms on to the constructivism pedagogy camp emphasizing the possibility of the learner to actively build an instructional visualization. If the learner tries to call a function, whose start-invariants are not valid, or in case a work-invariant would be injured by the call, the interactive visualization blocks the call with an error or warning notice. The notice includes the reason concerning the invariants.

It is also possible for the learner to follow steps that do not injure invariants, but also do not lead to the goal. Such steps can be undone individually.

Algorithm animation is different from ordinary animation, in that the final product is not simply a film which the user watches passively. Because an algorithm has inputs, its animation can be different each time the algorithm runs according to these inputs. Ideally the end user should be able to interact with an animation. Degrees of interaction can range along the scale depicted in Table 1 [Nap90] and [Nap96]:

Degree of Interactivity	Visualization systems	Example
None (Viewing Mode)	Still images	An illustration of the data is depicted in a picture.
	Animated pictures	The visualization runs like a video film. The viewer watches passively the visualization [BS81].
	Visualization with display adjustments	The user can start, stop, and step through the visualization, and adjust, i.e., the visualization speed.
	Visualization selection and arrangement capabilities (VCR)	The user can rewind the animation, and replay parts which were not understood on previous runs [TD95].
	Visualization with changing input, zooming and panning	The user can choose the input data for the topic being illustrated [Bro88b], or he can span and zoom to see the different part of the display [Sta89], [Sta90b] and [Bro88a].
	Visualization with interactive decision points	The user can change the data while the algorithm to be visualized runs, for example by dragging a data point to a different location and watching the effect of this change [BRM98] and [SER$^+$98].
very high (Experimenting Mode)	Visualization generated by students (visualization construction kit)	the composition and function of the eventual interactive visualization artifact is under the control of the user who is thus free to select and combine components such as data producer and encoding blocks according to his needs [KBKT99], [PED$^+$99] and [ESS$^+$99]

Table 1: Degrees of user interactions with a visualization system

2.4 Case Studies

Early efforts in algorithm animation in the late 1970's resulted in an educational film [BS81] presented at the 8th Computer Graphics Conference. The middle 1980's saw the development of systems [Bro88b], [BS84], [Bro88a] which allow a user to run algorithms and see animations interactively. Recent efforts have added color and sound [BK91], [JDE92], and [Sta90a], as well as the use of object-oriented programming [Bro91], [BN93] and the development of component-based framework for instructional visualization [SER+98], [BRM98], [KH98], [EFS99], [KBKT99], [SSvD99] and [ESS+99]. There is a strong pedagogical interest associated with instructional visualization, which can be used by students individually or in class demonstrations[SBL93].

In the following some of these systems will be discussed more deeply. The Discussion will not be exhaustive but will focus on techniques. here we will concentrate on questions that a designer of similar systems must face.

2.4.1 Sorting Out Sorting

"Sorting out Sorting", created by Ronald Baecker [BS81] and presented at Siggraph 1981 is the most well-known example of an early algorithm animation.

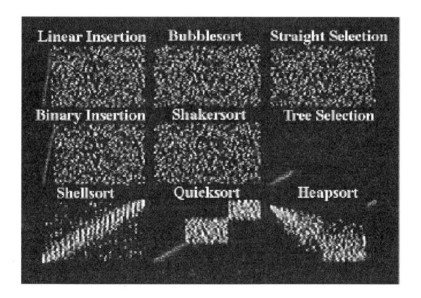

Figure 1: A snapshot from the final race in "Sorting Out Sorting"

It explains concepts involved in sorting an array of numbers, illustrating comparisons and swaps. The film illustrates and compares nine sorting algorithms as they run on different data sets. It ends with a race among the nine sorting algorithms, all sorting the same large random array of numbers. It shows the state of the array as a collection of dots in a rectangle;

each dot represents a number: x is the array index and y the value. Figure 1 shows a snapshot from the race. In a single screen, nine rectangles with moving dots vividly explain the behavior of nine algorithms. The audience can compare the $O(n^2)$ running times of insertion sort and quick-sort. The movements of the dots also convey the method used by each algorithm.

The film was very successful, and is still used to teach the concepts behind sorting. Its main contribution was to show that algorithm animation, by using images, can have great explanatory power. The film also demonstrated that tools were needed. The effort involved in its production (three years using custom-written software) stimulated research into making more general-purpose algorithm animation systems.

2.4.2 BALSA

Many current algorithm animation systems have their roots in Brown Algorithmic Simulator and Animator (BALSA) developed by Marc Brown and others in the middle 1980's. Its influence has been enormous, and by looking at its design one can learn about the problems that any algorithm animation system must solve.

BALSA [BS84] and BALSA-II [Bro88a] was developed in 1983 to animate algorithms interactively (first truly interactive visualizations) on special-purpose, networked, graphical workstations. In order to animate an algorithm, the algorithm designer augments an implementation of an algorithm with event signals which provide information to the animation routine, causing a display update. This work was especially compelling because students could step through an algorithm and watch the animation change as each line of an algorithm was executed, instead of merely playing back a pre-recorded animation. This work also illustrated that these animations were successful in helping students understand the material.

BALSA set standards with all following systems compared to it. Animations were built with predefined views that could be extended by a procedural programming language. The prepared graphical animations could be controlled by a VCR-like control panel (stop, start, speed control, replay, standard window control, panning, zooming). Animations could even be played backward. It was originally implemented in C, with the algorithms presented being in Pascal. Each algorithm could be observed from different directions at the same time, with BALSA being the first system to have algorithms rivaling against each other presented on the same screen. The source code of the running algorithm was also shown with the current line being highlighted. User inputs were recorded to enable others to redo the whole program session afterwards. BALSA originally ran on black and white monitors, with its successor BALSA II including color and sound being triggered at certain events.

2.4.3 Zeus

Zeus [Bro91] continued the ideas set forth in the BALSA project, but extended them to take advantage of strong-typing, parallelism and OO design paradigm. Again, algorithms were augmented with event signals. Libraries were developed to allow for more advanced animations including color, sound and later 3D graphics.

Zeus used as a starting point the Modula-2 implementation, porting it to Modula-3 enhanced it in a variety of ways. The essence of animating an algorithm in Zeus is to separate the algorithm from each view and to create a narrow interface, specific to each algorithm, between them. More specifically, an algorithm is annotated with procedure calls that identify the fundamental operations that are to be displayed. An annotation, called an interesting event, has parameters that identify program data. A view is a subclass of a window, with additional methods that are invoked by Zeus whenever an interesting event happens in the algorithm. Each view is responsible for updating its graphical display appropriately, based on the interesting events. Views can also propagate information from the user back to the algorithm.

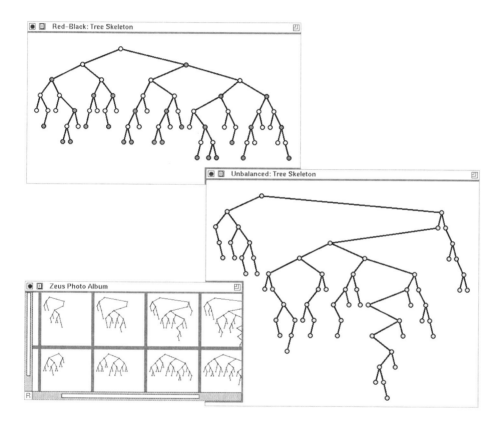

Figure 2: Snapshot of Zeus

Figure 2 is a snapshot of two binary search tree algorithm animations. In this case, the two algorithms are being run against each other on the same input data.

2.4.4 TANGO

TANGO [Sta90b] was developed by John Stasko in the late 1980's. It is a general purpose system for algorithm animation. Visualization technology so far developed needed to do animations by erasing complete pictures after slight changes were made and building them again showing the changes.

TANGO's framework consists of three parts:

- In the source code of the program, abstract operations and events are being defined to manage the animation.
- Animation scenes are being built.
- An animation control file is being originated that includes what animation scene has to be presented according to the interpreter hitting a certain operation or special event in the source code.

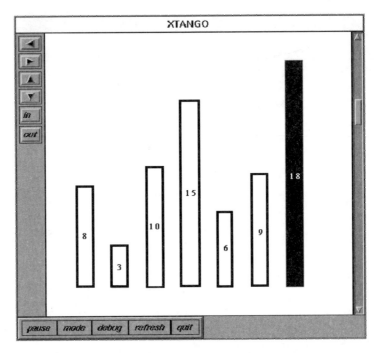

Figure 3: Snapshot of XTango

TANGO provides sophisticated facilities for the production of explanatory animations of algorithms. TANGO uses the "path-transition" paradigm for visualization [Sta90a] which simultaneously maps program data to graphical objects and program actions to animation actions involving the objects. The animation actions are defined using paths, arbitrary sequences of coordinates which are interpreted as points in some attribute space. The animation actions may be composed using several operators to generate various effects.

The user controls the animation via a VCR-like control panel (panning, zooming, pause, continue, speed control). The original version of TANGO ran on a BSD Unix workstation. The following decades saw the development of the XTANGO and POLKA [Sta92] systems, other major monolithic projects involving months or years of work by advanced students. Figure 3 illustrates Multiple frames from bubblesort in the xTango system.

2.4.5 Movie and Stills

An interesting approach to algorithm animation appears in Movie and Stills programs developed by Bentley and Kernighan [BK91]. These authors use the Unix text-filter paradigm. In this system, a program is animated by inserting output statements, and not function calls. Each output statement produces a textual description of the changes in the state of the program. This text must be written in a very simple language for describing shapes to be drawn and also identifying program events. In effect, by thus modifying a program, it will itself output a program which, if properly interpreted, results in an animation. One advantage of this approach is language-independence: the original program can be written in any language and run on any machine, since the animation information is communicated through simple ASCII output.

Two utilities are provided to interpret a program's output. The first one, Movie, animates the program on a workstation's screen. The user can pause the animation, speed it up or slow it down. The other tool, Stills, is a troff filter which allows frames from the animation to be included in printed documents. In a way, this system resembles Tango and other systems described above, which break the algorithm and animation into separate processes. The difference here is that the communication process occurs through pipes or intermediate files, and is in only one direction. This restriction makes it more difficult to animate programs that require graphical input, since the user interface must be written by the programmer.

2.4.6 The Exploratory Project

Andries van Dam and John Hughes from Brown University have been working on the Exploratory project [SSvD99]. One component of this project is to develop a toolkit for creating interactive illustrations in Java, which might, for example, augment the text and illustrations in an electronic book. None of these systems, however, attempts to automatically animate an algorithm created by a student, instead students are allowed only to view the results of a "reference" algorithm implemented and augmented with event signals by an expert.

One of the main advantages of the exploratory project is the reusable development process adapted through the use of the JavaBeans technology. The customizability issue of already developed applets is still not investigated. Thus applets may be developed easily (if the appropriate components were developed) but they can not be reused in different learn contexts and surely not in a desired context by another teacher.

2.4.7 HalVis

The animation-embedded Hypermedia algorithm Visualizations (HalVis) [HSN98], project at Auburn University is aimed at designing and evaluating algorithm visualizations as tools for self-learning, making use of component architecture advantages. The system works by taking an approach in which algorithm animation "chunks", coupled with context-sensitive multimodal explanations, are embedded in an interactive hypermedia information presentation system.

The system architecture [HNS98] can be depicted, describing the different modules according to certain features. These include having animations at multiple levels of granularity. Three distinct kinds of animations provide views of algorithm behavior at different levels of granularity. The first, called "conceptual view", is an animated real-world analogy intended to function as a scaffold and a bridge by conveying the essential features of the algorithm in familiar terms. The second, called "detailed view", is a detailed micro-level animation that focuses on specific algorithmic operations. The third, called "populated view", is a macro-level animation that shows the algorithm's behavior on large data sets. The detailed animation is chunked at multiple levels (at the level of a single instruction execution, at the level of a "pass" for algorithms that make multiple passes over data, etc.). Each chunk is presented in tandem with pseudo code highlighting and textual/aural explanations. The learner can elect to see the animation at any of the available chunking levels. The micro-animation is presented before the macro-animation, both of which are seen by the learner only after the animated analogy.

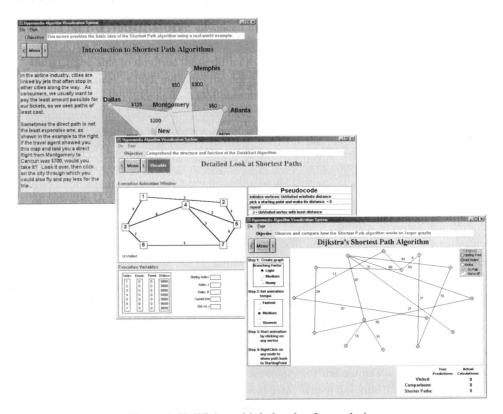

Figure 4: HalVis's multiple levels of granularity

HalVis is implemented using Asymmetrix Toolbook, and as of this writing, contains visualizations of four sorting algorithms and one graph algorithm. Each algorithm visualization in HalVis consists of the modules shown in Figure 4 and described above. The main disadvantage of HalVis is its platform dependency as well as the complexity in integrating the resulting visualization in an appropriate learn context.

2.4.8 Other Visualization Systems

Educational Fusion [Boy97] and [Aar99] is a system for developing and utilizing advanced interactive educational algorithmic visualizations on the world wide web. being developed at MIT. Educational Fusion (eFusion) allows educators to create interactive visualizations which require students to use problem-solving skills to implement solutions. The students can then immediately visualize their algorithm's output, and compare it to that of a hidden reference algorithm. This is an improvement over other educational systems which are limited to semi-interactive visualizations and simple question-and-answer forms. The main disadvantage of eFusion is that visualization can only be integrated in an appropriate learn system by a programmer.

Klein and Hanisch describe a system to realize an interactive computer graphics course [KH98]. Their system employs a concept to use component software (JavaBeans) to visualize different steps of a complex algorithm. However, no control structure is provided to group modules and to switch between different level of granularity.

Koutis chooses a component-based approach for a unified environment for the presentation, development and analysis of geoworlds [KBKT99]. His system also does not use the concept of granularity.

Mecklenburg and Burger describe a system to create component-based applets automatically from Estelle-specifications [BRM98]. Their System does not cope with the concept of granularity. Thus it is, like in other systems, not possible to integrate a visualization in different learning context and visualize different phenomena.

2.4.9 Lessons Learned

Most instructional visualization systems were developed in the belief that visualizations and animations (e. g. algorithm animations) would serve as effective supplements in educational purposes (e. g. lectures for students to learn about algorithms) [SBL93] and [HSN98]. This belief has a strong intuitive basis, since for example students have always had a relatively difficult time understanding abstract mathematical notions, especially when these include dynamics of how algorithms manipulate data, so concretizing these notions graphically and animating them to illustrate the dynamics ought to improve learning [PEKS00].

Instructional visualization helps the end-user to understand algorithms by following visually step-by-step their behavior or execution, such a process of visualization can be even more effective if interaction with the presentation of the data is supported [SL98] and [MPG98]. Usually an animation depicts abstractly how the program is executed [Mye90], by choosing illustrations that materialize algorithm or topic data.

Figure 5 summarizes the characteristics of the discussed instructional visualization systems and gives an overview of the lessons learned. At the beginning, instructional visualization system were monolitic. The interaction was mostly done through VCR-like control panel. During their evolution these system have been improved to support better illustration and even granularity at different presentation levels. Instructional visualization systems were further improved to provide some explanation facilities. Some of these systems even provided users with more than one view of the data, which we should consider while developing interactive visualizations. An important aspect learned from the surveyed systems is to provide users with identical views of different algorithms manipulating the same data. This is necessary because students should concentrate on the acquisition of information through direct comparison of different solutions and not on learning new interaction and graphical user interface elements.

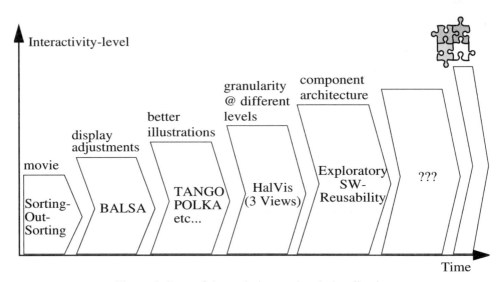

Figure 5: State of the art in instructional visualization

Even though these systems inspired us with some ideas, they still have some deficiencies. A lot of these visualization systems have been developed without regard to software engineering in terms of reusability (req #1). The animation of JPEG or MPEG serves as a good example: Even though both compression schemes use the Discrete Cosine Transform (DCT), and the Huffman encoding, a reuse of a component coming from an already finished animation of JPEG can in most cases not be used to visualize a step of the MPEG-compression process. Another drawback of today's visualization systems is their platform (req #3) and context dependencies (req #2). Instructional visualizations are often monolithic, which makes them difficult to confront and address changing user requirements and knowledge, and therefore their Integration in appropriate multimedia learning systems is still difficult (req #2). Finally most of these systems do not support the collaboration facilities (req #5), and if then they do not provide different views of the same visualization in a collaborative environment (req #6).

2.5 Summary

This Chapter tried to convey the state of instructional visualization, to inform the prospective algorithm designer the options available, whether he/she is designing a new system or using an existing one to create animations.

To draw a conclusion of the survey, many of these systems have been developed without regard to software engineering in terms of reusability and platform independency. This situation typically results in low-end visualization functionality, poor designs and big development costs. The discussed systems are monolitic, they are not flexible enough so as to confront and address changing user requirements and knowledge. None of them allows a visualization to be usable in a variety of context. Thus in most of the cases a user cannot integrate a visualization in an appropriate learn context. Furthermore users are only provided with one view of the data. The use of visualizations in multiuser interactive environment is mostly not supported.

Recapitulating, it is obvious that lot of the above claimed requirements are not fulfilled. This work tries to alleviate these deficiencies while retaining the desirable characteristics of those systems. The next Chapter discusses reusability issues in instructional visualization.

Chapter 3 Reusable Instructional Visualization Modules

Rapid advancement in computer, communication, and presentation technology produces new forms of media and communications which can be used to increase the quality of educational documents visualizing complex technical problems. To help students learn difficult concepts, interactive learning software needs specific capabilities for simulation, visualization, and real-time data collection, as well as tools for analyzing, modeling, and annotating data. Such interactive, dynamic representations are meanwhile the core content of educational learning modules. These representations have to be combined flexibly with many kinds of contexts: diverse classroom presentations, tutorials, experimentation notebooks, and standardized assessments (req. #2). In order to achieve that goal, the standardization of so-called *Learning Objects* has become an important issue.

As stated in the specification of IEEE's Learning Objects Metadata (LOM) [Gro00], "a learning object is defined as any entity, digital or non-digital, which can be used, reused or referenced during technology-supported learning". Examples of learning objects include multimedia content, instructional content, instructional software, and software tools, referenced during technology supported learning. In a broader sense, learning objects could even include learning objectives, persons, organizations, or events. A learning object is not necessarily a digital object; however, the remainder of this work will focus on learning objects that are stored in a digital format.

Learning content forms the basic blocks for education and training, whether delivered to the learner or produced by the learners themselves. Reusability of content (req. #1) is important in terms of saving money and production time and allows resources to be produced collaboratively in a modular way.

The notion of reuse is traditionally considered important for computer applications, and is divided in two broad different categories: reuse of software components (code) and reuse of information. Reuse of software components can be defined as the ability to use a piece of code in different contexts or different systems, whereas reuse of information, means that a data item (simple or complex, traditional or multimedia) is used in different applications, or in different parts of the same application within different context.

In the reminder of this Chapter the first two requirements (req. #1 and req. #2) concerning reusability and customizability will be addressed. The software reusability issue is discussed first followed by a discussion of using metadata to enhance the indexing and finding and therefore the reuse of developed interactive multimedia learning resources in different context. To support the customization requirement (req. #2), a new classification scheme for metadata for learning purposes will be presented.

3.1 Software Reuse in Learning Systems

Software engineering is a an engineering discipline which is concerned with all aspects of software production from the early stage of system specification to system maintenance after it has gone into use [Som00]. Software Engineering can therefore be seen as the design of a framework to enable diverse functionalities to co-exist and share resources on a computer or a network [RDK+99].

One of the main challenges contemporary organizations increasingly face is generated by the existing gap between the complexity of software development and the state-of-the-art of software engineering tools. While computing power and network bandwidth have increased dramatically over the past decade, the design and implementation of complex software in general and educational software, in particular, remain expensive and error-prone [FS97]. Despite some gains, the software industry still faces long development cycles, which often result in software products that do not address business problems adequately. One of the main causes is that much of the cost and effort are generated by the continuous rediscovery and reinvention of core concepts and components. Software reusability has therefore become a goal in software engineering for decades, especially in educational institutions, where the software developer team changes constantly and each student, i.e., solves his assignments and exercises in a different way. In this thesis, Krueger's general view of software reuse is adopted [Kru92]:

> "Software reuse is the process of creating software systems from existing software rather than building them from scratch."

Reusing software is not a simple assignment [JF88], [Opd92]. It started with Niklaus Wirth's Modula-2 programming language [Wir90], which was designed to facilitate the team development of large software engineering projects. The module structure is designed to compartmentalize a program into independent modules which can be developed, modified, and used in any combination without worrying about interference with other parts of a program.

Important progress towards achieving the goal of reusable software was made during the 1980s with the emergence of software engineering lifecycles. In order to define the steps for the creation of software and to establish transition criteria to systematically progress from one step to another, models for the software development process were derived from other engineering activities [Boe88]. The major advantage of software process models is their guidance regarding the order in which to fulfil certain tasks [Sam97].

A further step towards reusability was the introduction of the object-oriented paradigm [WR92]. Object-Oriented Programming (OOP) [Boo94] has the potential of increasing the reuse of software components through inheritance and object composition mechanisms. As a result, the software industry has moved towards embracing object-oriented technology because of its potential to significantly increase developer productivity through reuse [Som00]. Still, all the object-oriented techniques provide reuse only at the level of individual, often small components. The more complex problem of reuse at the level of large components that can be adapted for individual applications was not addressed by the OOP paradigm itself, but rather by the Component-Oriented Programming (COP) [Szy97], [Sam97].

3.1.1 Object-Oriented Programming

The difficulty in factoring out common functionality for reuse, extending and specializing functionality, and maintenance overhead [tal96], has forced the software community to look for new approaches to software programming other than traditional procedural programming languages. While procedural design techniques centre on the functions of the system, Object oriented techniques centre on the data (objects) of the system [Boo94]. Booch defines object oriented programming as follows:

> "Object-oriented programming is a method of implementation in which programs are organized as cooperative collections of objects, each of which represents an instance of some class, and whose classes are all members of a hierarchy of classes united via inheritance relationships"

The object-oriented paradigm presents techniques to facing the challenge of building large-scale programs. It originates with Simula, which was initially dedicated to solving simulation (model building) problems. Since then, OO technology has been exploited in a wide range of applications including databases, operating systems, distributed computing, and user interfaces. The main benefits that confer such a broad range of applicability to the object-oriented approach as presented in [AC96] are:

- *The analogy between software data models and physical data models*:
  The analogy with a physical system model has proven to be useful in the process of developing a software model. It makes the analysis of the problem more efficient.
- *The resilience of the software models*:
  Unlike the approach advocated by procedural languages, which emphasizes the use of algorithms and procedures, the design of OO systems emphasizes the binding of data structures with the methods to operate on the data. The idea is to design object classes that correspond to the essential features of a problem. Algorithms, factored in methods and encapsulated in objects, form natural data abstraction boundaries. The main consequence of encapsulation is that it helps focus on modeling the system structure rather than trying to fit a problem to the procedural approach of a computer language.
- *The reusability of the components of the software model*:
  Objects are naturally organized into hierarchies during analysis, design, and implementa-

tion and this encourages the reuse of methods and data that are located higher in the hierarchy. Furthermore, this property generates all the other advantages associated with software reuse including low maintenance overhead, high productivity etc.

One of the main advantages of the OO paradigm is that it promotes the reusability of software components. [JF88] and [Opd92] have identified those attributes of object-oriented languages that promote reusable software:

- *Data abstraction*:
  refers to the property of objects to encapsulate both state and behavior. The only way to interact with an object and to determine an object state is by its behavior. Thus, data abstraction encourages modular systems that are easy to understand.
- *Inheritance*:
  is the sharing of attributes between a class and its subclasses. It promotes code reuse, since code shared by several classes can be placed in their common superclass to be inherited and reused.
- *Polymorphism*:
  allows an object to interact with other different objects as long as they have the same interface. It simplifies the definition of client objects, decouples objects from each other and allows them to vary their relationships to each other at run-time. For example, the expression "a+b" will invoke different methods depending upon the class of the object in variable a. Operator "+" in this case is overridden in each class.

Object-oriented languages have introduced a significant revolution in programming techniques. However, even if the programming job is made easier as the work is performed at a higher level of abstraction with objects and class libraries, the programmer is responsible for providing the structure and the flow control of the application. Therefore, reusability is achieved mainly at the class level and only rarely at a higher level, e.g., structural level.

Source code is most commonly reused; thus many people misconceive software reuse as the reuse of source code alone. Recently source code and design reuse have become popular with class libraries, application frameworks, and design patterns. One aspect of concern deals with the way web-based educational systems have been built. Success and wide-spread diffusion of a system are believed to depend strongly on the ideas of software engineering and especially reuse that have been taken into account. It should be noted that software reuse is still an emerging discipline. It appears in many different forms, from ad-hoc reuse to systematic reuse, and from white-box reuse to black-box reuse. Following approaches can be characterized:

- Ad-hoc or Non-systematic approach
- Design Patterns
- Software Architecture
- Frameworks
- Component Software

3.1.2 Ad-hoc or Non-Systematic Reuse

Scavenging code fragments from existing software programs and using them in the development of a new software system is unsystematic, although effective approach to reusing software source code and system design [Kru92] and [Sam97]. In this ad-hoc and unsystematic scenario reused components are code fragments taken from various locations of other software systems rather than self-contained, tested and documented components from a repository. Ad-hoc and unsystematic software reuse is sometimes called the principle of "cut and paste" and can be characterized by the following two aspects:

- Reuse of code: Code-blocks of an existing software system are being copied into the new system.
- Reuse of design: Large code-blocks of an existing software system are being copied into a new system, erasing many details but keeping the template or pattern of the old system.

Using the unsystematic approach, there is no abstraction involved in scavenging. The developer is therefore forced or inspired to understand many implemented details in the reused code [Fre97] and [Sam97]. Therefore, this way will most often imply a lot of effort and can not be recommended.

3.1.3 Design Patterns

Software design patterns [Coa92], [GHJV97], and [Pre95] address the software reusability issue by offering a possibility for capturing and expressing design experience. Patterns capture knowledge about software construction that has been gained by many experts over many years. Design Patterns were derived from ideas put forward by Christopher Alexander [AIS+77], who suggested that there were certain patterns of building design that were common and that were inherently pleasing and effective. Design patterns provide an efficient means of studying and later reusing the designs of experienced software engineers. Patterns can help to improve productivity by shortening the learning curve for novice and intermediate programmers by yielding simpler systems. In contrast to methodologies that *tell* us how to do something, design patterns *show* us how to do it [GHJV97].

Design patterns identify, denominate and abstract the main aspects of recurring behavior or structures of software. That way the definition of a so called "pattern" includes the description of the overlaying problem and the essence of its solution, which may be reused in different settings. A design pattern is not a detailed specification. Rather one may think of it as a description of the accumulated experience. Since abstract solutions including the description of the involved elements and their specific contribution to solving the problem are being described in design patterns, they can aid in the enhancement of the productivity of programmers. [GHJV97] defines Pattern as:

> "Each pattern describes a problem which occurs over and over again in our environment, and then describes the core of the solution to that problem, in such a way that you can use this solution a million times over, without ever doing it the same way twice."

In our daily programming, we encounter many problems that have occurred, and will occur again. The question we must ask ourselves is how we are going to solve it this time. Documenting patterns is one way that you can reuse and possibly share the information that you have learned about the best way in solving a specific program design problem. Essay writing is usually done in a fairly well defined form, and so is documenting design patterns. According to [GHJV97], each design pattern has four essential elements:

- *Pattern name*:
  is a handle that can be used to describe and nomenclature design problems. It is a meaningful reference to the pattern.
- *Problem/Issue:*
  describes when the pattern may be applied.
- *Solution*:
  explains the different parts of the design solution, their relationships and responsibilities. It provides an abstract description of the design problem, and also a general arrangement of elements that will solve it.
- *Consequences*:
  describe results and trade-offs of applying the pattern. This is used to help designers understand whether or not a pattern can be effectively applied in a particular situation.

Through this uniform structure are design patterns easy to understand and use. Patterns represent distilled experience which, through their assimilation, convey expert insight and knowledge to inexpert developers. They help forge the foundation of a shared architectural vision, and collective of styles. Once a solution has been expressed in pattern form, it may then be applied and reapplied to other contexts, and facilitate widespread reuse across the entire spectrum of software engineering artifacts such as: analyses, architectures, designs, and implementations. Due to the type of the design patterns, software reusability takes place mainly on cognitive level. It concerns only semi formal descriptions of certain problems, which can occur in software projects. Possible design solutions can be inferred from the catalog of design patterns. If a suitable pattern is found, then this can be applied to the problem definition. With the help of the class diagrams of a design pattern the structure of the solution can be transferred to the analysis and Design diagrams of the object-oriented modeling. Thus design patterns are settled in the reuse hierarchy over the source code reusability but under software architectures and Frameworks.

3.1.4 Software Architectures

The best-known software architecture is the MVC-Model (model-view-controller). This user-centered (event-driven) approach was originally a basic design paradigm in Smalltalk [GR89], therefore discussed extensively in the Smalltalk literature, and moved on to be the standard architecture in software systems requiring graphical user interfaces. The principle of MVC is based on the separation of responsibilities. The presentation of the information (view) is unlinked from the applications' functionalities (model) and the processing of the user inputs (controller) [GS88]. Following the MVC-model represented in Figure 6, three logical areas can be identified:

- A *model* (database) is an object the state of which is to be changed. The model itself does not have any knowledge about its graphical presentation in the user interface. It therefore does not accept any messages sent out by the controller which are specific for a certain user interface. This property guarantees that the model is independent from a specialized form of presentation. The model sends out messages to the controller and receives such.
- A *view* (Presentation) is an object which is responsible for the visualization of particular aspects of a model. A view sends messages to the controller and receives messages from the controller.
- The *controller* (application domain) as an abstraction of the control procedures is an object which controls the communication between a model and its corresponding view. The controller sends messages to other views as well as to the model and receives messages from both.

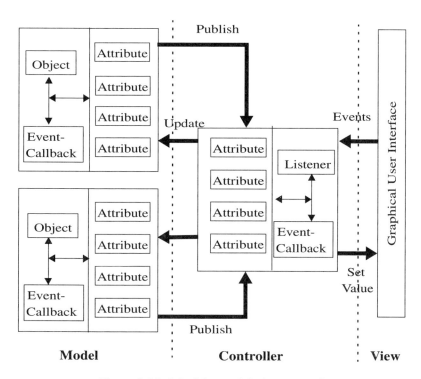

Figure 6: Model of the model-view-controller

The advantages of using the MVC-architecture can be seen as:

- Uncouples application data from presentation
- Enhance / optimize model without affecting view
- Customizable Look & Feel
- Multiple views into a single model

By decoupling the data (model) and the way the data is represented (view) multiple differing view objects can present the same model data. No changes need be made to the model as view representations change or new ones are created. The MVC-model can be simplified as shown in Figure 7. Thus the use of the MVC-paradigm has to be considered for the development of instructional visualization in order to have different views of the same application, and thus use it according to different user requirement and background knowledge (req. #2) or to share the same instructional visualization with diverse views (req. #6).

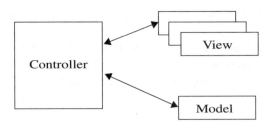

Figure 7: Simple MVC-model

3.1.5 Object Oriented Frameworks

An object-oriented framework (OOF) is essentially the design of a set of objects that collaborate to carry out a set of responsibilities in a particular problem domain. OOFs attracted attention from many researchers and software engineers for their ability to facilitate the reuse of larger components at a larger granularity [tal96] and [BMMB]. A framework provides a generic design. It may also provide facilities (user interface, storage, etc.) that are useful to all applications. A framework is a partial (incomplete or generic) solution to a set of similar applications. The task of a developer is to take this incomplete solution and add the necessary code to create a complete application. A framework represents a part of an application. This part is designed by domain experts who has coded and tested it.

Frameworks have been defined for a large variety of domains such as: process control systems within particular application domains [BMA97], operating systems within computer science, financial systems [BCK+97], multimedia [PLV97], and many others. As more experience has been gained in developing OO frameworks, several research projects have been conducted to study their impact in the software development effort and to identify their problems and difficulties [JR91], [Mat96], [SF97], and [SSS00a].

Different definitions of the term "framework" can be found in the literature. Johnson [JR91] defines a *framework* as a set of objects that collaborate to carry out a set of responsibilities for an application or subsystem domain. Mattson [Mat96] uses the definition of a (generative) architecture designed for maximum reuse, represented as a collective set of abstract and concrete classes; encapsulated potential behavior for subclassed specializations. A widely accepted definition is given by Johnson and Foote [JF88]:

> "A framework is a set of classes that embodies an abstract design for solutions to a family of related problems, and supports reuses at a larger granularity than classes"

The key terms in this definition are:

- *Set of classes*:

  The set of classes refers to a number of object oriented classes corresponding to the essential features of a problem domain

- *Design*:

  The design of an application defines the overall structure of an application, its partitioning into classes and objects, the key responsibilities thereof, how the classes and objects collaborate, and the thread of control

- *Abstract design*:

  An abstract design is a design in which some of the components (classes) are abstract. Abstract classes are written with the expectation that concrete subclasses will add structure and behavior typically by implementing abstract operations.

- *Solutions for a family of related problems*:

  The solutions to a family of related problems usually have common elements. They can belong to particular business units (such as data processing or cellular units) or application domains (such as user interfaces or real-time avionics).

- *Reuse*:

  Software reuse is the use of existing assets in some form within the software product development process. More than just code, assets are products and by-products of the software development life cycle and include software components, test suites, designs, and documentation

- *Granularity*:

  Granularity in this definition refers to the level of reuse. Low granularity reuse is the reuse of components while higher granularity reuse refers to design or analysis reuse.

- *Usability*:

  Usability refers to the quality or state of being usable. There are many factors that contribute to the usability of a framework such as: adaptability, robustness, learning, performance, standardization, help, etc.

A framework usually defines the overall structure of all the applications derived from it, their partitioning into classes and objects, the key responsibilities thereof, how the classes and objects collaborate, and the thread of control. The developer is only responsible for customizing the framework to a particular application. This consists mainly of extending the abstract classes provided with the framework. A framework provides the structure for a set of similar applications. A developer creates a particular application by adding the behavior to the framework necessary to differentiate it from other similar applications.

An important role of frameworks is the regulation of the interactions that the parts of the framework can engage in. By freezing certain design decisions in the framework, critical interoperation aspects can be fixed. A framework can thus significantly speed the creation of specific solutions out of the semi-finished design provided by the framework.

Classification of Frameworks

There are many types of frameworks on the market, ranging from those providing basic system software services such as communication, printing, and file systems support, to the very specialized ones for user interface or multimedia software components. Although the underlying principles are largely independent of the domains to which they are applied, a classification of frameworks by their scope is sometimes useful [FS97], [Som00]:

- *System infrastructure frameworks*:
  Their primary use is to simplify the development of portable and efficient system infrastructure including operating systems, communication frameworks, and frameworks for user interface. Being used internally within the organization, they are not typically sold to customers directly [SF97].
- *Middleware integration or support frameworks*:
  Their primary use is to integrate distributed applications and components. They enhance the ability of software to be modularized, reused, and easily extended. Examples of middleware frameworks include message-oriented middleware and transactional databases [OH98].
- *Enterprise application or domain frameworks*:
  Their primary use is to support the development of end-user applications and products directly and therefore represent the base of enterprise business activities. They address different types of applications in a broad application domain such as telecommunications, avionics, manufacturing, education, and financial engineering [BCK+97]. In spite of the cost of developing and/or purchasing, enterprise frameworks can provide a substantial return on investment since they support the development of end-user applications and products directly. Enterprise JavaBeans (EJB), Lotus, and SAP are examples of such frameworks.

Traditional frameworks fully concentrate on classes and inheritance. However, there is no reason why a framework could not emphasize on object composition instead. As implementation inheritance, even in the presence of reuse contracts, tends to require knowledge of the superclass implementations, it is often called whitebox framework. Object composition, on the other hand, if based on forwarding rather than delegation, merely relies on the interfaces of the involved objects. It is therefore often called blackbox framework. Frameworks can therefore be classified according to the techniques used to extend them. From this perspective, frameworks range along a continuum between the following two extremes:

- *White-box or architecture-driving frameworks*:
  rely heavily on OO features such inheritance and dynamic binding. The framework is extended either by inheriting from framework base classes or by overriding pre-defined hook methods [Szy97], [Sam97]. A white-box framework defines interfaces for components that can be plugged into it via object composition. However, the difficulty of using object-oriented white-box frameworks resides in the fact that they require in-depth understanding of the classes to be extended. Another weakness, specific to subclassing in general, is the dependence among methods: e.g., overriding one operation might require overriding another and so on. Subclassing can lead in this case to an explosion of classes [Mat96].
- *Black-box or data-driven frameworks*:
  are structured using object composition and delegation rather than inheritance. They

emphasize dynamic object relationships rather than static class relationships. New functionality can be added to a framework by composing existing (provided) objects in new ways to reflect the behavior of an application. The user in this case does not have to know the framework in-depth details, but only how to use existing objects and combine them. Black-box frameworks are therefore generally easier to use than white-box frameworks. On the other hand, black-box frameworks are more difficult to develop since their interfaces and hooks have to anticipate a wider range of potential use cases. Due to their predefined flexibility, black-box frameworks are more rigid in the domain they support. Heavy use of object composition can also make the design harder to understand. Nevertheless, many framework experts expect an increasing popularity of black-box frameworks, as developers become more familiar with techniques and patterns for factoring out common interfaces and components [Mat96], [Szy97], and [Sam97].

These two categories presented above are extreme cases because in practice a framework hardly ever is pure white-box or black-box, or has only called or calling components [Opd92]. In general, in a framework, inheritance is combined with object composition. In the case of a white box framework, the application programmer has to implement the derived concrete classes. In contrast, a black box framework provides all these concrete classes and the user is responsible for choosing the appropriate ones and combining them to obtain the functionality required by the application.

Object-oriented Framework takes the evolution of software engineering from procedural programming to class libraries one step further by introducing black-box frameworks. Black-box frameworks carry the concept of code reuse one step forward by providing a structure for components, which will be discussed next.

3.1.6 Component Software

After several years from its conception, object technology has proven to be useful in solving real-world problems. However as more object oriented solutions are developed and deployed, it is becoming evident that object orientation alone cannot cope with the increasing complexity of today's software applications. Object-oriented methodology provides valuable methods to create self-managed entities through data encapsulation and object abstraction [Boo94]. The promise of object technology is code reuse by reusing objects in class libraries. It is true that class libraries can indeed increase a programmer's productivity through the reuse of existing classes. However, objects form only a part of an application: they totally fail to capture the structure (flow of control) of the application. It turns out that many applications, especially in the same domain, share similar structures. Different programmers use different techniques to capture and implement these structures. As a result, such structures are not reused through usual object-oriented techniques.

Component-based software is the latest paradigm in software development [Szy97] and [Sam97]. Components are reusable, off-the-shelf software units that can be purchased from component vendors [Eng97]. Different components of the application can reside in different operating systems and can be implemented in different languages [Sam97]. Legacy code can be wrapped within components and used with the rest of the system. New technologies in hardware and software can be immediately leveraged on by implementing new components in the new environments. A component of the application can be versioned independently of other components. There exists no need to recompile and redeploy the entire application [Szy97]. Figure 8 shows our view of a software component. A component provides a customization interface to customize its behavior at design time. It exposes to the world its events, methods, and properties. Furthermore a component may contain other components and / or classes, and it allows packaging [FE99].

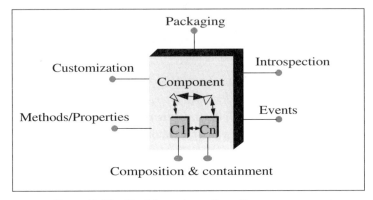

Figure 8: The blackbox view of a software component

A component can be defined as a unit of software. This unit should be large enough so that the component can be packaged and deployed. However, the unit should be small enough so that it can be maintained and upgraded. A component has the following properties:

- *Deployable*:
  A component is an off-the-shelf, packaged pieces of software that can be purchased from a vendor.
- *Maintainable*:
  A component is small enough so that it can be easily maintained and upgraded.
- *Functional*:
  A component is large enough so that it behaves in a desired, useful manner.
- *Specificity*:
  A component is designed to perform a very specific task. It represents a piece of an overall application. This piece can be fine-, medium-, or coarse-grained.
- *No direct communication path to other components*:
  A component should not directly communicate with another component. This lack of direct communication is essential for components to be maintainable and upgradable. Moreover, it allows them to be used in distributed environments. This property does not imply that a component cannot invoke the services of another component. Rather, it emphasizes that the actual mechanism to invoke the service is done by another entity (an object bus or a framework).

- *Self describable*:
  A component can describe the services it provides to the rest of the system. This description is usually provided through a declarative, implementation-independent interface definition language.

The above characterization of components provides a mechanism to partition an application into components. Each component provides a very specific functionality. It also describes itself to the rest of the infrastructure so that other components can access its functionality. The description is accomplished via a declarative language, which essentially separate the interface of a component from its implementation. This separation is critical in order for the component to operate in a distributed environment. The mechanisms that provide this data are called reflection and introspection. Reflection is therefore the ability to obtain information about the fields, constructors and methods of any class at run time. Introspection is the ability to obtain information about the properties, events and methods of a component. In fact introspection uses reflection to obtain information about a component.

According to this contemplation, it seems that a software component represents the higher degree of reusability (req. #1) and allows easy customization (req. #2).

3.2 Component-Based Development Methodology

An ideal scenario of software engineering is to build applications by putting high-level components together [EFS99]. If any desirable components are not found, they have to be composed out of existing lower-level components. The components have to be implemented in a certain programming language [ESS+99]. Components software are autonomous, reusable computational software entities playing the role of primitive buildings blocks whose behaviour can be determined (programmed) at end-user. They are designed so that they may be combined with other components in configurations defined by end-users and behave as composite constructs.

Component-based design (CBD) methodologies are based on many of the same principles as object-oriented design and use the same diagrams and notations as many OO methodologies. It uses the Unified Modeling Language (UML) notation and diagrams [RJB99], [Qua99]. In the following the CBD methodology is presented [Spa00].

Component-based software systems are designed at two levels: In specification, a developer understands and describes a problem. This process includes analysis and design; the result is a potential solution for a software application. The solution might be expressed in graphics or text using a particular notation, such as UML. An implementation is the realization of the specified solution. This process is accomplished using a programming language or other development tools. This approach means that the products of the development process will include software, as well as diagrams, models, and other specifications.

The steps that are traditionally associated with software development [Boe88]: analysis, design, and implementation, still exist in the CBD method. They are categorized under the headings of either specification or realization. The design step actually crosses the boundary between specification and realization because some tasks are designing the specification, and some tasks are designing implementation details. As depicted in Figure 9, CBD is an iterative process. As one moves from the specification to the realization stage, and as the design and development moves from the analysis to the implementation phases, it is possible to go back and refine things that occurred in earlier phases [Spa00].

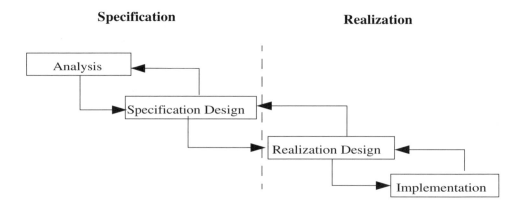

Figure 9: An overview of the component-based development method

Furthermore, specification components are independent of realization technology. This provides a developer the flexibility to use a given specification component in different applications or environments. For example, UML specification can be used in any object-oriented development environment. A developer might use C++, Java, and VisualBasic implementations. The value of the component is therefore not exclusive to its software implementation, but to its specification. Component design decisions are driven by a variety of factors that help define the range of component granularities. Usually components are encouraged to be larger rather than smaller. However larger components by nature have more complex interfaces and represent more opportunity to be affected by change. The larger the component, the less flexible is the structure of the system. Thus a balance is struck, depending upon the level of abstraction, likelihood of change, complexity of the component, and so forth [Hop00]. The principles of cohesion and coupling are the factors. Minimizing the coupling of the system tends to work against good cohesion. Next section discusses the granularity issue of component software.

3.2.1 Granularity of Instructional Visualization

Components can be as large as whole applications such as a pdf viewer. But examples of small components include many of today's available Graphical User Interfaces (GUI) components also called *widgets* that are available from many development organizations. They are often implemented as JavaBeans or ActiveX components. Another important aspect of components is specificity. The more closely a component matches the design, the less modification is required. Naturally, the number of components increases as they become more specific.

Large components also denoted as "coarse-grained" components for interactive visualization illustrate only some of the intermediate computations that take place within an algorithm [GSvD99]. Coarse-grained components are appropriate for certain concepts, mainly for those courses where self-contained algorithms and data structures are taught. However, many concepts and topics in multimedia communication are combinations of small concepts that provide parts of a theoretical framework for larger algorithms. The visualization of JPEG [SN95] or MPEG [MPFL97] serves as a good example: Even though both compression schemes use the Discrete Cosine Transform (DCT) and the Huffman encoding, a reuse of a component of an animation of JPEG can in most cases not be used to visualize a step of the MPEG-compression process, if the illustration is coarse-grained. Coarse-grained animations are very useful in demonstrating the final concept, but are hard to use in teaching the individual ideas that are part of that concept.

The best granularity of the developed modules is, therefore, strongly correlated with the domain being addressed and varies widely between concepts. The goal with the modular model is to strive for the smallest possible scope for each concept. The requirements for a component-based framework for instructional visualization can be identified as interactive and supportive to the learner.

Interaction implies that the learner is guided in the sense that he can get feedback if problems emerge. Assuming that the handling of the toolkit itself is intuitive such problems can only result from the difficulty of the topics to be learned. The difficulty of an algorithm to be animated can result either from the knowledge of the learner which might not be sufficient to understand the topic or from the amount of information presented by the animation. If the user's knowledge is not sufficient to understand parts of an algorithm we offer two possibilities to create the corresponding knowledge: a user can read a short explanation of the part of the algorithm he currently executes or he can invoke the Chapter of the textbook explaining the underlying theory in depth. The latter includes search functions to get a more specific way of explanation. The processing of an insufficient knowledge of a learner is performed in a traditional way by using hyperlinked multimedia documents.

The second problem however, the density of the presented information is to be considered by the use of levels of complexity. The idea behind a level of complexity is that a user can reduce the information density of a part of an algorithm by splitting the part of an animation he/she is currently using into a particular number of steps equivalent to a smaller information density, which can be understood easier. This technique of mastering complexity has been known since the ancient times and is known as the principle of divide et conquer (divide and rule) [Dij79]. When designing a software system, it is essential to decompose it into smaller parts, each of which may then be refined independently. This process is shown in Figure 10. While C stands for complexity, the upper index denotes the level, the lower the number of a component.

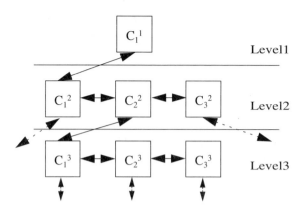

Figure 10: Levels of complexity

3.2.1.1 Top-down versus bottom-up design

The chief means for dealing with complexity, in software engineering as well as other technical disciplines, is the notion of abstraction. In our context, abstraction involves separating the details into hierarchical levels, whereby one level hides the details of the levels below from the level above. The universal consensus is that abstraction is a vital tool in software design. What is less agreed upon is whether it is better to develop the abstractions starting at the highest level and working down, or starting at the lowest level and working up. This so called "top-down vs. bottom-up" debate has raged for quite a while; successful software engineers and computer scientists wholly devoted to one or the other.

In the top-down approach, the total problem is broken down into a nested series of subsidiary problems until a level is reached at which components can be implemented. This approach allows to deal with parts in relation to the whole, and offers the most effective way of maintaining structural and functional consistency across the entire interface.

The virtues of bottom-up design include the following. It is easier to think in terms of low-level (bottom) entities; they tend to be more concrete, hence easier to conceptualize. So, say the advocates of bottom-up design, it is better to start from the bottom, where the complexity is manageable, and work upward, with each successive level relying on the abstractions provided by the level below. The design of each level, in essence, therefore merely involves piecing together the components and services provided by lower levels, enabling the management of complexity at successively higher levels of the hierarchy. When the services provided by a given level are sufficient to solve the entire problem, you create one final "top" level and you are done.

The bottom-up design philosophy has its drawbacks, however. Perhaps the major difficulty it presents is in determining what the lowest level components should be. How can it be known exactly; what services are required by higher levels if they haven't been designed yet? Low-level entities of the software may be designed, only to be found later that they are inadequate, or unnecessary for solving the problems encountered at higher levels.

A third approach is the so called "meet-in-the-middle" design methodology, whereby it is intended to work top-down and bottom-up simultaneously, with the two ends of the design hopefully coming together somewhere in between. While seemingly combining the benefits of both the top-down and bottom-up methods, experience has shown that successfully joining the high-abstraction levels with the lower levels can be quite difficult. In real life, the top and bottom often do not come together as nicely as planned.

Finally, we considered a methodology that involves top-down design with concurrent top-down implementation. When components at a lower level of abstraction are deemed necessary, we design their interface and implement them as "stubs". These stubs need not provide meaningful functionality; they merely acted as placeholders around which the rest of the abstraction level was implemented.

A great advantage of the modular approach is that several fine-grained visualizations can serve as stand-alone visualizations illustrating individual ideas. They can also be reused and combined with others in order to visualize a more complex topic. Granularity here refers to the level of detail that we seek to visualize in order to understand gross or fine-level process dynamics or details.

3.2.2 Component Characteristics

Component consists of at least one object. Objects encapsulate state and behavior. State corresponds to attributes which are usually implemented with instance variables. Changing the attributes (instance variables) of an object requires changing its code.

A dynamically customizable component needs a scheme that does not require code changes, thus a way to add a new variable or remove existing attributes on the fly. To be uniquely identified, each attribute is associated with a unique key. These keys are used to access, alter, modify or remove attributes at runtime.

Properties are aspects of a component's appearance and behavior that can be observed or changed (or both) directly. They represent the conceptual attributes. Whenever a property stereotype is used, two operations, "get" and "set" are automatically defined, which get and set the corresponding property attribute. Subtypes of property, such as Read-only property and Write-only property, may also be defined in a similar way. For every Property, there is exactly one Get and one Set method, which operate on the property:

- The `get` methods takes no arguments and returns the value of its corresponding Property.
- The `set` methods takes exactly one argument whose value must be a subtype of the type of the value of its corresponding property.

The postcondition of `set` is that the value of the property is the same as the argument passed to `set`. In some cases, properties can have extra characteristics such as being constrained by certain conditions, raising events after a change, or permitting vetoes just before a change.

Several ways exist to ensure the inter-component communication. Among others are the direct method calls, which lead to the fact that the execution context of the called method lies at the caller side (caller component) and the event driven communication mechanism, which leaves the execution at the receiver side. Event driven inter-component communication is, therefore, preferred because components are then decoupled at run-time. Thus they can be developed more easily as autonomous units, which is as the same time a prerequisite of component software development process.

A trigger of an event initiates a chained reaction, in which the appropriate methods are executed to compute a new state and/or value of a component. Events provide an alternative to (synchronous) method invocations for any type of communication between components in which "background notifications" are appropriate. That is, components providing one or more computational services can acknowledge and handle other services on an event-driven, or asynchronous, or "logical interrupt" basis. In this event-driven paradigm, the source and target orientation is a matter of context. A component can be a source for one type of event and a target for another. An event occurrence is typically followed by some type of event notification. The event notification process passes along pertinent event-related data to each registered target in a specialized event object. For every event, there is exactly one register and unregister operation

- Register and Unregister operations have exactly one parameter: To register an event the `addEventListener()` method is needed, while to unregister it the `removeEventListener()` method is needed.

Therefore, a component consist of a set of state and shared attributes or properties, a set of elements responsible for the creation of the user interface and also of a set of methods to define relationships and interdependencies among state/shared variables and events. These characteristics are listed below:

- A set of state-attributes: The state of a component is at any moment fully determined by the values of its state-attributes. A component needs only to store its state-attributes to fully reproduce its current state at a later time. State-attributes can have arbitrarily complex data types.
- A set of shared-attributes: The values of these attributes can be exported and/or imported to/from other component via corresponding communication channels. shared-attributes can also be state-attributes. Shared-attributes can have arbitrarily complex data types.
- A set of communication channels comprising the component interfaces, which handles the data exchanges among components and directly or indirectly affect state and/or shared-attributes. Thus each component has:
  - An input side, which defines the interface for inputting data or control information. This also defines the pins type for the purpose of composition.
  - An output side, which provides a reusable implementation for attaching a component's output to another component's input.
- A set of graphical user interface elements, which directly affect state and/or shared attributes, in the case of graphical component.
- A set of methods that define the relationships and interdependencies among state/shared variables and events coming from:

- The user, through user interaction if any.
- Other components through communication-channels.

In the following component assembly will be discussed.

3.2.3 Component Assembly

A component assembly is a static configuration of components. Unlike a component specification, which defines a component in isolation, an assembly description focuses on how components are "wired" together. This introduces the notion of a connector, which joins together component pins (connection points, such as methods or properties) and causes them to interact in a precisely defined way. The specification of the components (including their pins) and the connectors of an assembly together completely define the behavior of the assembly.

Pins are connection points at which components can be coupled to each other using the appropriate connectors.

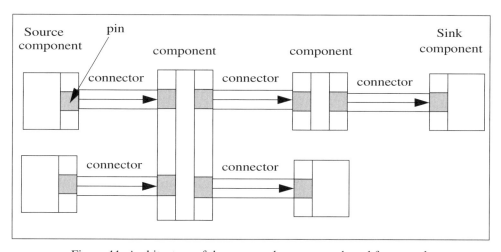

Figure 11: Architecture of the proposed component-based framework

A connector is a way of plugging together compatible pins of one or more components. Familiar connectors include method invocation and sharing variables. The component architecture presented here allows components to have properties and events, as well as methods, and so require special connectors to wire up property pins and event pins. All connectors support connection and disconnection of component pins. Many connectors are directional, distinguishing between source pins and sink pins to indicate that information flows in one direction only (from source to sink). A directional connector model can be defined similarly to the undirected connector model shown above, by distinguishing the connection management operations for source pins and sink pins. The invariants relating the attributes and operations are:

- `ConnectOperation` takes one pin of a component and one source or sink attribute of a connector as its arguments. Its post condition is that the value of the source or sink attribute specified is the pin argument.
- `DisconnectOperation` takes one pin of a component and one source or sink attribute of a connector as its arguments. Its post condition is that the value of the source or sink attribute specified is null.

The component assembly process is not only necessary during the development stage, but also for the development of a construction kit according to the constructivist learn theory. Student can use already pre-defined and pre-fabricated component, plug them together and study the resulting outcome, without the need to learn any programming language as presented in 4.3.6. In such an environment user can change the behavior of a visualization by omitting certain steps or by adding or exchanging components.

3.2.4 Components for Instructional Visualizations

The most important component-software solutions currently available are Microsoft's ActiveX [Dav96], Apple's LiveObjects [App95], and Sun's JavaBeans [Eng97]. DCOM (ActiveX) offers a great variety of programming languages like C, C++ and Visual Basic.

Language	Pascal	Modula2	C	C++	Smalltalk	Java
Simplicity and regularity	yes	yes	no	no	yes	yes
static types	yes	yes	yes	yes	no	yes
dynamic types	no	no	no	yes	yes	yes
static objects	yes	yes	yes	yes	no	no
full type safety	no	no	no	no	yes	yes
	unsafe variant record					
inheritance	no	no	no	yes	yes	yes
multiple inheritance	no	no	no	yes	no	yes (Interface)
garbage collection	no	no	no	no	yes	yes

Table 2: Comparison of some programming languages supporting component software

ActiveX can be used in the Internet and makes use of drawing libraries of the underlying operating system. Major disadvantages of ActiveX are its missing platform-independency (req #3) as well as the lack of a multilingual support. The latter is quite important if the system has to be used by learners from different countries.

Apple's OpenDoc is quite similar to ActiveX despite the missing ability to be used in the Internet. On the other hand OpenDoc's LiveObjects have the important property of cross-platform-interoperability.

Sun's JavaBeans [ON98'] are platform-independent and can interoperate over different platforms. Furthermore Java offers a multilingual support and can be used in the Internet. A minor disadvantage is the concentration on Java thus prohibiting the use of other languages such as C++.

Architecture	DCOM	OpenDoc	JavaBeans
Name of Component	ActiveX	Live Object	Bean
Creator of component	Microsoft	Apple	Sun
Imaging	Use of the underlying operating system drawing libraries		Java AWT / SWING
Programming languages	C, C++, Visual Basic,..	C, C++,...	Java
Cross-Platform	no	no	yes
Cross-Platform-Interoperability	no	yes	yes
Multilingual-Support	static	static	dynamic

Table 3: Comparison of different component framework

From the comparison above (Table 2 and Table 3) it is clear that JavaBeans promise the most effective way to create a component-based software for animations, visualizing multimedia and network technology. Another main reason for favoring JavaBeans over ActiveX is its backwards compatibility. While it is not possible to carry more than one ActiveX version installed on one machine at a time, on the one hand, it is possible and easy to have more than one Java version installed on one machine, on the other hand.

3.2.5 Component Repositories

Potential reuse of component software in general and for learning components in particular can be enhanced by providing access to component repositories spread over networks. A component repository is a database for the storage and retrieval of reusable components. A repository can be seen as the link between development for reuse and development with reuse as well as the use of already developed learning software. Those it contains components with all relevant information about them, including their documentation, range of use, design, interaction with other components and classification. The chance that a learning software component will be reused depends on the availability of potentially reusable components in the repository, but it also depends on the mechanisms provided to describe, search, and find a component within the repositories.

An important aspect of the component description is the description of its variability. To this end, components carry generic parameters being kind of "placeholders" for specific properties that are left variable in the component. A generic parameter can, e.g., be a place-holder for a simple string value denoting a language choice, a specific algorithm from a set of given choices, or in the most complex case, a placeholder for arbitrary input. The entirety of parameters together with the ranges of allowed values express the spectrum of possible variants that can be generated from a component (although in most cases not all combinations of parameter settings will be sensible and allowed). The next section discusses the possibilities to describe instructional components in a useful way.

3.3 Metadata in Learning Systems

IEEE's Learning Object (LO) model is characterized by the belief that independent chunks of educational content can be created that provide an educational experience for some pedagogical purpose. With regard to Object-Oriented Programming (OOP) [Boo94] and Component-Oriented Programming (COP) [Szy97], [Sam97], [Hop00] this approach assumes that these chunks are self-contained, though they may contain references to other objects, and they may be combined or sequenced to form longer (larger, complex, other) educational units. These chunks of educational content may be of any type, interactive (e.g., simulation) or passive (e.g., text, picture or simple animation), and they may be of any format or media type. The modular development process of educational multimedia content from the software engineering point of view was discussed in the previous section.

Another requirement for learning objects is related to tagging and metadata. To be able to use and reuse (req. #1) such objects in an intelligent fashion, they must be labelled to what they contain, what they communicate, and what requirements with regard to their use exist. To integrate learning objects in an appropriate learn situation, they should be able to adapt to changing user background knowledge (req. #2). A reliable and valid scheme for tagging learning objects in general and interactive visualizations in particular, is hence necessary. Next definitions and goals of using metadata is discussed.

3.3.1 Definition and Goals

Metadata are "data about data", they are descriptive information about resources for the purpose of finding, managing, and using these more effectively. they can be seen as a system of labels whose purpose is to describe a resource or object's characteristics and its objectives [IMS00].

Metadata are a way to describe information resources and contain data about their form and content. A resource is anything you make available to others. It may be a book in the library, a document, a video or music clip, a multimedia content, an instructional content, an instructional software and software tools no matter if it is physically available on the Internet or not.

Metadata are important because they form the single web that knits an information system together, tying system components and system software to the data so the data can be processed, stored, searched, retrieved, and distributed.

It should be noted that metadata are not only for educational purposes relevant. There exist a lot of engineering and other fields where metadata plays a major role. The origin of metadata may be found in the library world. Every book in a library is described by means of author, title, publisher, publication date, and abstract. In this case, the library cards contain the metadata on the books. If we are looking for a specific book, the library cards have the information needed. One could say that metadata structures the information we need on a resource.

The starting point for the work presented thereafter is the existing technologies, standards, and on-going initiatives with regard to multimedia educational metadata. The Dublin Core (DC) [DC00] Metadata Element Set, Educom's Instructional Management System (IMS) [IMS00], the Alliance of Remote Instructional Authoring and Distribution Networks for Europe (ARIADNE) [ARI00], and IEEE's Learning Object Metadata Working Group 12 (LOM) [Gro00] are the most important initiatives dealing with metadata for computerized learning purposes. These initiatives are closely related to the Resource Description Framework (RDF) [RDF00], the Warwick Framework [Lag], and to other activities of the World Wide Web Consortium. Metadata classification will first be presented, followed by some application areas of metadata. Diverse metadata for learning resources will then be discussed.

3.3.2 Application of Metadata

Metadata for learning content, has been under development within a number of international organizations over the past few years [GEM00], [IMS00], and [ARI00]. The purpose of metadata is to provide a common means to describe things (electronically) so that "learning objects" (however they are defined) can be self defined, searched, and found. Learning content is only one area of metadata application [DM91]. Metadata is also actively being developed in all aspects of Web-based content and commerce [Ora98]. Today, the Internet abounds with resources. Looking for a specific topic or resource, probably hundreds or thousands of resources will be found. Most of them do not meet the requirements at all. A search most commonly ends up with an enormous list of hits where the main part is not applicable. The advantages of using metadata in general are [Gro00]:

- to summarize the meaning of the data, i.e., what is the data about
- to allow users to search for data
- to allow users to determine if the data is what they want
- to prevent some users such as children from accessing data
- to retrieve and use a copy of the data, i.e., where do I go to get the data
- to instruct how to interpret the data like format, encoding, encryption

To providers or publishers metadata is interesting because it eases the discovery and access to their resources to reuse it (req. #1). Making a resource available to others is one thing. But what is the point if the resource cannot be discovered? Ensuring that users can locate the resources should have a high priority.

For the person searching for material metadata is quite helpful. It optimizes the search situation by narrowing down the search result list to real applicable resources. The resources that are located will always be presented with minimum information such as creator, subject, type, format, and identifier. The metadata provider must enter this kind of information. If the resource meets the searcher requirements, the location of the resource will inform him as to where to obtain it.

We need the metadata to decide whether we would like to apply a certain resource; whether there are certain conditions involved with the usage; and whether there are certain technical requirements [Ora98]. Metadata can be stored separately from the resource, but it can also be stored together with the resource. Metadata on the Internet, for instance has to be machine-readable and machine-understandable. Metadata stored separately from the resource can be located, e.g., in a database. Metadata stored together with the resource can be placed, e.g., in the top of a document. There are several activities in progress to develop a tagging scheme for learning objects, including the Dublin Core, the Instructional Management System (IMS) project, the Alliance of Remote Instructional Authoring and Distribution Networks for Europe (ARIADNE), and the IEEE Learning Technology Standards Committee (LTSC). More initiatives exist, but it is not within the scope of this work to present all initiatives, nor is it useful to involve them all. Some of the metadata standard initiative will be discussed next.

3.3.3 Metadata Standard

Before explaining our classification in the next section, we will describe some of the metadata initiatives that have helped us in our work, starting with general purpose and ending with specific ones, dealing with metadata for learning resources.

3.3.3.1 Dublin Core

The Dublin Core initiative [DC00] was an early effort to standardize what the core tags for general information objects should be, and has been remarkably successful with regard to the fact that most standardization efforts of learning content start with Dublin Core. The Dublin Core is now separately investigating the special case of educational objects, somewhat independently of other ongoing work.

The Dublin Core set is not designed for multimedia objects or learning aspects. However, Dublin Core uses widely accepted semantics [Ora98], which means that the element names are commonly understood. It is a very user-friendly metadata model as it is short and simple, and most important, it is flexible and extendable. The Dublin Core set consists of 15 elements. These elements are: Title, Creator, Subject, Description, Publisher, Contributor, Date, Type, Format, Identifier, Source, Language, Relation, Coverage, and Rights. The new Dublin Core sub-elements are: Date (metadata last modified), Date (resource last modified), Price, Requirements (software and hardware), and Size (physical size in bytes).

The main characteristics of the Dublin Core that distinguish it as for description of electronic resources are:

- *Simplicity*:
  the Dublin Core is intended to be usable by experienced and non-experienced cataloguers. Most of the elements have a commonly understood semantics of roughly the complexity of a library catalogue card.
- *Semantic interoperability*:
  promoting a commonly understood set of descriptors that helps to unify other data content standards increases the possibility of semantic interoperability across disciplines.
- *International consensus*:
  recognition of the international scope of resource discovery on the Web is critical to the development of effective discovery infrastructure. The Dublin Core benefits from active participation and promotion in countries in North America, Europe, Australia, and Asia.
- *Flexibility*:
  although initially motivated by the need for author-generated resource description, the Dublin Core includes sufficient flexibility and extensibility to encode the structure and more elaborate semantics inherent in richer description standards.

Dublin Core is still having some model details refined, but compared to Instructional Management System and Learning Object, Dublin Core is further along in the development process than the others. Since IMS, ARIADNE, and IEEE LOM Working Group all consider multimedia objects, educational and commercial aspects, these models are used for extending and adapting Dublin Core.

3.3.3.2 ARIADNE

The Alliance of Remote Instructional Authoring and Distribution Networks for Europe (ARIADNE) is a resource and technology development project of the 4th Framework Program of the European Union. ARIADNE's primary goal is to foster the share and reuse of electronic pedagogical material, both by universities and corporations. It is not the intention to describe the human actors involved in the process of education and training. Neither it is the intention to define the representation format for the metadata sets. ARIADNE has two goals for the metadata work:

- The indexing work carried out by humans should be as easy as possible.
- Looking for relevant pedagogical material should be as easy and efficient as possible.

ARIADNE also requires that the metadata system works in a multilingual and multicultural environment (see section 4.3.5). However, their solution to this problem is to make the system neutral to both the language of the original document and the language of the metadata. Their reason for this approach is that mechanisms ensuring multilingual interoperability are difficult to design and implement. ARIADNE is co-operating with IMS and IEEE-LOM in order to come out with standardized learning metadata. Both of these initiatives will be discussed next.

3.3.3.3 IMS

Instructional Management System (IMS) project [IMS00] is supported by the Educom National Learning Infrastructure Initiative. The initial development occurred as a collaborative effort among educators, information science professionals, and technologists interested in creating a standard system for accessing on-line resources plus making it easier to learn via the Internet. IMS defines metadata as "descriptive information about learning resources for the purposes of finding, managing, and using these learning resources more effectively".

The IMS Project is developing and promoting open specifications for facilitating on-line activities such as locating and using educational content, tracking learner progress, reporting learning performance, and exchanging student records between administrative systems. With these specifications, IMS-Project wants to increase the range of distributed learning opportunities and to promote the creativity and productivity of both teachers and learners in this new environment. The goal of the IMS project is the wide spread adoption of specifications that will allow distributed learning environments and content from multiple authors to work together. The IMS technical specification provides general guidelines and requirements developers must write in order to create interoperable content and management systems.

The IMS partnership is creating a specification that is intended to become a de facto industry standard that will be distributed and implemented without first going through a formal standard process. The rationale for this approach is based on a realization that time to market is extremely important in this environment, and that de facto standards represent a much faster means of disseminating a design into the marketplace than do formal standards. The IMS has now begun the standardization process together with ARIADNE. The two projects have worked closely on a common metadata proposal for the Learning Object Metadata Working Group of IEEE described in the next section.

3.3.3.4 IEEE-LOM

The mission of IEEE Learning Technology Standards Committee (LTSC) working groups is to develop technical Standards, Recommended Practices, and Guides for software components, tools, technologies, and design methods that facilitate the development, deployment, maintenance, and interoperation of computer implementations of education and training components and systems. LTSC has been chartered by the IEEE Computer Society Standards Activity Board. Many of the standards developed by LTSC will be advanced as international standards by ISO/IEC JTC1/SC36 Information Technology for Learning, Education, and Training.

IEEE-LTSC P1484.12 Learning Object Metadata Working Group (LOM) tries to specify syntax and semantics of Learning Object metadata, defined as the attributes required to adequately describe a Learning Object. Learning Objects are defined here as any entity, digital or non-digital, which can be used, reused or referenced during technology-supported learning [Gro00] and [EGFS00]. Examples of technology-supported learning include computer-based training systems, interactive learning environments, intelligent computer-aided instruction systems, distance learning systems, and collaborative learning environments.

The Learning Object metadata standards focuses on the set of properties needed to allow these Learning Objects to be managed, located, and evaluated. The standard accommodates the ability for locally extending the basic properties as defined through data elements and entity types, and the properties can have a status of obligatory (must be present), optional (may be absent), conditional, or not allowed. Relevant properties of Learning Objects to be described include type of object, author, owner, terms of distribution, and format. Where applicable, Learning Object Metadata may also include pedagogical properties such as; teaching or interaction style, grade level, mastery level, and prerequisites. It is possible for any given Learning Object to have more than one Learning Object Metadata set.

IEEE's specification of Learning Object's Metadata (LOM) defines the following nine categories [Gro00] for metadata of a learning object which will be described in detail because of their importance for the presented work [EFS01]:

- *General*:
  General metadata, such as the title, language, structure, or description of a Learning Object (LO).
- *Life Cycle*
  Status, version, and role of a LO.
- *Meta MetaData*
  Metadata describing the metadata used for a LO.
- *Technical*
  All technical information about a LO, such as the format, the length, browser requirements, etc.
- *Educational*
  Information about the educational objective of a LO, such as interactivity, difficulty, end-user type, etc. (details see below).
- *Rights*
  Commercial use and ownership of a LO.
- *Relation*
  Implements a concept similar to hypermedia links to be able to refer to other LOs.
- *Annotation*
  Used to provide additional, eventually more detailed information about a LO.
- *Classification*
  Defines different purposes of a LO, together with its location within a taxonomy of keywords.

Each of these categories groups appropriate metadata fields of a specific aspect. With regard to the intention of this work, the category educational is especially important [EFS01]. This category contains several types of tags:

- *Interactivity type*:
  covering the information flow between resource and user, with restricted values *active*, *expositive* (passive), or *mixed*.
- *Learning resource type*:
  describing the specific kind of resource (which can be a list, prioritized), and allows any

terminology. Recommended values are *exercise, simulation, questionnaire, diagram, figure, graph, index, slide, table, narrative text, exam,* or *experiment.*

- *Interactivity level*:
  defining the degree of interactivity, and ranges from *very low*, through *low, medium, high*, to *very high.*
- *Semantic density:*
  can store the same values, and is used to define a subjective measure of a resource's usefulness relative to size or duration.
- There are categories for *intended end users* (teacher, author, learner, manager), *context of use* (an open vocabulary, but examples include primary education, secondary, higher education, different university levels, technical schools, etc.), *typical age range, difficulty* (again, a range from very low to very high), and *typical learning time.* Also included are a text description of the resource, and a language choice from the international standard codes.

The standard supports security, privacy, commerce, and evaluation, but only to the extent that metadata fields will be provided for specifying descriptive tokens related to these areas; the standard will not concern itself with how these features are implemented. IEEE-LOM expects these standards will conform to, integrate with, or reference existing open standards and existing work in related areas.

3.3.4 Lessons Learned

The efforts discussed above, allow to describe any learning objects, such as, documents, images, and simulations in such a way that an intelligent search engine is able to find and to use them in a local or distributed working process and learning situation (req. #1).

When studying and considering these standards, an important disadvantage becomes obvious: Due to the history of the development of metadata, static resources, such as images or text documents can be described properly. Unfortunately, an appropriate description of dynamic resources, for example animations, is feasible only to a limited extent. The reason is that dynamic multimedia objects can process input parameters, generate output parameters, and also work internally with data which cannot be described with traditional metadata schemes. These changes are necessary to match the learning goals of a user and to reuse dynamic multimedia content in a different context (req. #2). This aspect will be discussed next.

3.4 Metadata and Interactive Visualizations

As discussed in Section 3.2, properties, events, and methods are the building blocks of instructional visualizations. For these components to be used intelligently, they must be labeled as to what they contain, what they teach, and what requirements exist for using them, for instance configuration data or metadata. Therefore, modifications of the configuration data change the object model. In turn, changing the object model alters the system behavior.

Thus a need exists for a reliable and valid scheme for tagging these learning objects. Before presenting the new tagging scheme, a classification of metadata will be given first.

3.4.1 Metadata Classification

According to the InfoQuilt project [inf00] metadata can be classified into two categories: content-dependent and content-independent metadata:

- *Content independent metadata*:
  it does not capture the information content of the document. It describes, e.g., location, date of creation, etc.
- *Content dependent metadata*:
  it captures the information content of the document and thus depends directly on the document content. There are two types of content dependent metadata.
  - *Content descriptive metadata*:
    the content of a document is described in a manner which may not be directly based on the contents of the document.
  - *Domain specific metadata*:
    is a special case of content-descriptive metadata typically represented in an attribute-based manner where the attributes used to characterize documents are domain specific in nature.

All of the methods used to classify metadata make use of metadata in its traditional sense of describing data to facilitate search activities of the data (in general the documents) they describe. That is, the metadata descriptors are associated in a fixed way with the data sets and as granular as defined initially. However, metadata can also be seen as parameters that are passed to some object of a system in order to change its behavior as well as providing information, which will help search engines [EGFS00]. In order to change the behavior (dynamic property of a resource allowing it to be integrated into a desirable context) of an object, it should be possible to change parameters on the fly. For this purpose metadata for dynamic content are needed, extending the static nature of metadata in the traditional sense [EFS01]. Thus following classification arise:

- *Static metadata:*
  We call metadata that are used to create universal and widely applicable descriptions of objects, which may not change the behavior of the described object "Static metadata". Static metadata are purely descriptive metadata that are not used to control anything. Examples of static metadata are textual descriptions like comments of some base data IEEE-LOM [Gro00] and Dublin Core [DC00]. Static metadata is directed at the end-user who knows how to read and interpret it.
- *Dynamic metadata:*
  We suggest the use of the new term "dynamic metadata", describing the possibility to adapt the content of an object according to the value given in the description and the ability to change the value of a parameter of a given object in order to change its behavior. Dynamic metadata are metadata that controls its base data and is operational in a general sense of the word. It not only describes base data but defines how the base data is to be

interpreted and used. In object-oriented systems, metadata become metaobjects, which unite the metadata with the associated control functions of the base data.

As an example of dynamic metadata, we will in Section 4.4.3 examine the simulation of the CSMA/CD protocol (Ethernet). To be able to explain Ethernet properly, specific problems have to be addressed, for example the collision of packets on the bus, or the shortframe problem.

The key idea behind dynamic metadata is that the same visualization can be used to explain different problems, if it is configured by parameters. In the following we will explain the data structures for dynamic metadata in detail, but to motivate the problem, we provide an example here. A part of the data structure could be a field "PROBLEM", addressing a specific parameter configuration of a visualization. Concerning the visualization of Ethernet, changing the value of the metadata field "PROBLEM" (being represented in the program as a property) from "Collision" to "Shortframe" may change the whole behavior of the algorithm to be visualized.

3.4.2 Meta-metadata

The high road of metadata is data about metadata, or, for short, meta-metadata. Meta-metadata are data that describe (and in case of dynamic meta-metadata control) the operations of metadata. This is more common than one might think. The definition of modeling languages like UML are meta-metadata. Also, the modeling language extensions of UML for data warehousing are meta-metadata. Because metadata are data about data, and this data may be dynamic or static data, each of these data may have metadata. As a consequence dynamic metadata is recursive.

3.4.3 Metadata Specification for Interactive Learning Objects

As described in Section 3.3.4 the metadata descriptors are associated with the data sets in a fixed way. Their granularity is as defined by the original metadata author. A great drawback is that the application of metadata is used in a static way with respect to the content. A first observation is that such metadata cannot describe interactive visualizations adequately. Moreover, it cannot influence the multimedia content itself, because metadata usually contain universal and widely applicable descriptions of objects.

Figure 12 illustrate the traditional way of tagging a learning object using, i.e., the IEEE-LOM scheme. In this traditional tagging process a lot of descriptions can exist simultaneously in order to describe a specific content. To describe n resources, one may need m descriptions, where $m > n$ is. An ideal situation for the use of metadata is to have exactly one description for every content ($n = m$).

As mentioned above, the categories of LOM Base Scheme could cover diverse meta information about the instructional visualizations. LOM can be used to search, navigate as long as static learning objects are used. However, the particular potential of interactive visualizations, in other words their flexibility and adaptability, can only be exploited to a limited extent. For example, some interactive visualizations can be used to illustrate different scenarios or different parts of an algorithm, depending on the input parameters. The same learning object can be reused in a different learning context, according to the way it is configured by parameters. The question that arise know is how can an instructional visualization illustrating several behaviors be tagged?

An intuitive and simple answer would be: To use an interactive visualization in n arbitrary different scenarios, it should be parametrized, stored (with the appropriate configuration), and therefore tagged (assuming the ideal tagging scenario) n-different times.

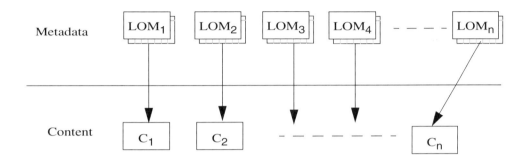

Figure 12: Ideal traditional metadata tagging process

Another problem with such a situation is that the number of the scenarios an interactive visualization can illustrate depends not only on the number of the attributes (parameters) a visualization components has, but also on the number of values this parameter is allowed to have. If for instance an interactive visualization contains three attributes, each of them may have five different values, this visualization can, therefore, illustrate 15 different situations. Thus, following the standard metadata tagging scheme, the person, who is in charge of the tagging process needs to describe the visualization fifteen different times in order to use it in all possible scenarios it offers. This is somehow unacceptable and unrealistic, even when using templates, since for instance IEEE-LOM has about 65 fields (see Appendix B).

Yet another problem, encountered with today's metadata is that of automatically generate a lesson. LOM is among others not enough to use, The reason is LOM does not for instance specify the physical size of a learning resource in means of pixels or dots (the physical size of LOM describe the size in Bytes and not in pixels) there is a need for some other elements like, i.e., the height and the width of an interactive visualization to be integrated into a dynamically generated lesson.

Recognizing the high cost in tagging and using instructional visualizations does not help us unless we are able to reduce it. Parametrization of interactive visualizations can be done off-line or on-line. Using traditional metadata assumes that the parametrization of interactive visualizations is to be done off-line. To achieve an on-line customization, we propose the use of dynamic metadata as an extension of the static IEEE Learning Objects Metadata.

3.4.4 Extension of IEEE's LOM

Initially we wrote informal textual or UML descriptions capturing the important information about a representative sample of interactive visualizations that we wanted to describe and use in different context. After reviewing these descriptions using LOM draft 4 and after that draft 5 which required extensive discussions with the whole team for clarification, we went through the textual and UML descriptions and identified LOM elements in which the information expressed could be captured. Where we failed to find LOM elements for an item of information we extended the LOM, either by expanding on the vocabulary of an existing element or by creating an entirely new element under a new category. Where new elements were needed we searched other repositories to find metadata that we could use. Among others we searched the Gateway to Educational Materials (GEM) [GEM00] and the Advanced Distributed Learning (ADL) Initiative [ADL00]. Dynamic metadata can be understood as an extension of IEEE's Learning Object Metadata. This category groups the information to define the behaviour of dynamic learning objects or instructional visualizations. The scheme of dynamic metadata follows the generic format of <property, values, value type>. According to the LOM specification [Gro00], this scheme is illustrated in Figure 13.

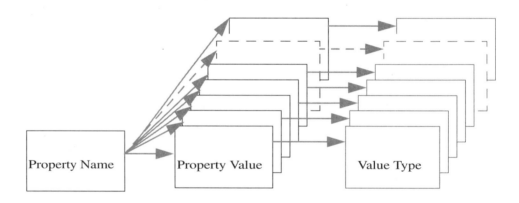

Figure 13: Generic scheme of dynamic metadata

3.4.5 Flexible Visualization

It is essential that a visualization is flexible enough to confront and address changing user requirements and knowledge. It should also be versatile, and usable in a variety of contexts. While often, a visualization will not fit the needs of a particular user "off the rack", it can be tailored to do so when certain "alterations" are done. The educator may convert an algorithm implemented by the developer to a series of animation sequences by mapping algorithm variables, specifying animation actions, and associating execution points in the algorithmic chain to perform the desired animation. He uses dynamic metadata. This leads to the fact that it is easy to integrate animations in the appropriate context.

Back to our usage scenario presented in the introduction, the developer, who is in charge of writing the appropriate code of the algorithm to be animated can reuse (req. #1) software developed according to the component-base framework presented in Section 3.2. The educator becomes the designer of the visualization to be shown. He can customize the learning object in order to visualize a desired behavior, which is appropriate for the course to be taught. Thus he uses and reuses already developed instructional objects accompanied with dynamic metadata (req. #1 and req. #2). The student, for instance becomes the end-user of the customized animated algorithm. The advantages of dynamic metadata can be summarized as follow:

- Allows to tag a resource once and use it in different scenarios (req. #1)
- Allows the tailoring of interactive visualization according to user needs (req. #2)
- Allows the integration of interactive visualization in an appropriate learn context (req. #2)

3.5 Summary

One of the key problems in developing learning software systems in general and interactive instructional visualization units in particular is the integration of user requirements changing over time. Learning systems must be flexible in that they must be easy to adapt to new and changing user requirements.

The aspects of software engineering with respect to developing reusable learning units was discussed in this Chapter. Various aspects have to be considered in order to make a learning unit reusable. Developing a visualization learning unit as a component software ensure a higher development reusability, but on the other hand it can be very difficult to integrate it in an appropriate learn context. The reason is, teachers often prefer to have the opportunity to do some tailoring of materials for their own purposes, without having to do the basic development.

Describing learning component software in component repositories is important for effective finding and retrieval. Various tagging techniques exist to describe learning objects in general. The metadata descriptors addressed in the literature are associated in a fixed way with the data sets. Their granularity is defined by the original metadata author. A great drawback is that the application of metadata is mainly limited to the offered fields where metadata are used in a static way with respect to the content. A first observation is that such metadata cannot describe dynamic multimedia content adequately. Today's metadata standard can not influence the multimedia content itself, because metadata usually contain universal and widely applicable descriptions of objects. In my point of view, the usage of dynamic multimedia learning objects, such as interactive visualizations, requires a new sort of metadata, which must be dynamic in order to facilitate the adaptation of for instance the Input/Output (I/O) behavior of a dynamic multimedia content. That is why this work is proposing to rethink the way we look at metadata, and suggesting a new metadata classification, namely, static and dynamic.

In the next Chapter we will discuss Multibook, a project founded by the German Ministery for Education and Research (BMB+F). The results of this Chapter will be introduced in a component-based framework enhanced with dynamic metadata. This framework is the skeleton for developing instructional visualizations and integrate them into the Multibook.

Chapter 4 Multibook:
The Personal Multimedia Book

Multibook[1] [Mul00] is a web-based adaptive hypermedia learning system for multimedia and communication technology, focused on providing end-users with specific lessons tailored to a targeted group. These lessons are created using a knowledge base of multimedia elements, especially interactive animations.

The Multibook system can be devided into multimedia content development tools, multimedia content description and processing tools, and multimedia knowledge base. As discussed in Chapter 3, this work focuses on the development and customizing process of instructional visualizations, therefore a component-based toolkit for the development of instructional visualizations "iTBeanKit", will be addressed together with an adequate set of dynamic metadata in order to integrate interactive multimedia content within the Multibook. Multimedia content description and processing tools varies from the tagging of the content, like, for instance, the LOM Editor described in Section 4.2.2 to course generators, user control tools and a test environment which are out of the scope of this work. Some of these tools are described in [SRH+00], [PEKS00], and [SRH+01].

During the implementation, both the platform independency requirement (req. #3) as well as the usability requirement (req. #4) were considered. This Chapter ends with a parade lesson implementation showing how the diverse parts of this work fit together. Software metrics indicating the degree of software reusability (req. #1) achieved are given. Evaluation studies dealing with the customization (req. #2) of instructional visualization as well as their usability (req. #4) are also presented.

4.1 The Multibook System

The aim of Multibook is to offer different lessons for different users. There are mainly two possible ways to accomplish this: either by storing a huge number of compiled lessons (the

---

[1]Multibook was funded by the German Federal Ministry for Education and Research (bmb+f) between 1997 and 2000. It was developed by Darmstadt University of Technology, the Fern-Universität Hagen, University of Illinois, University of Ottawa, Intelligent Views Software and Consulting GmbH, and Springer-Verlag.

disadvantage of this approach is not only the amount of storage but also the static character of such lessons) or by dynamicaly generating the lessons individually for each user. Since the dynamic composition also facilitates the exchange or modification of information, Multibook follows the second approach. In [See01] four dimensions for the user profile of Multibook were defined. Initially, the profile is filled with the demands and preferences of the users. While the users are working with Multibook, the system keeps track of what information they have already seen / learned, what additional material they have demanded to see, the results of the tests, etc.

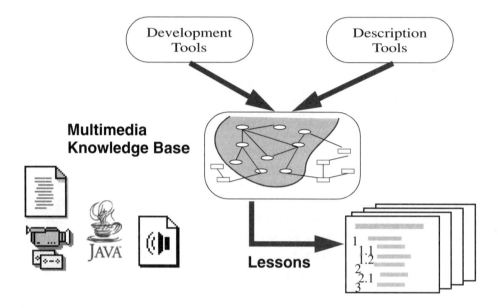

Figure 14: Multibook System

4.1.1 Overview

Multibook's knowledge base consists of two separated knowledge spaces: the ConceptSpace and the MediaBrickSpace [SSR+99a], [FS00]. The ConceptSpace contains a networked model of learning topics [SSR+99c] and uses approaches well known from knowledge management. The knowledge topics are interconnected via semantic relations. The media bricks stored in the MediaBrickSpace of the system are atomic information units of various multimedia formats. These units are interconnected via rhetoric relations [MT87]. Each media brick is described using the IEEE's Learning Object Metadata (LOM) scheme [Gro00]. In the following we refer to media bricks as learning objects. Although both information spaces are separated, each learning object can have a relation to one or more related topics. The separation of the aforementioned spaces is the way in which Multibook generates adaptive lessons, because for each topic a set of media bricks (texts in different granularity, animations,

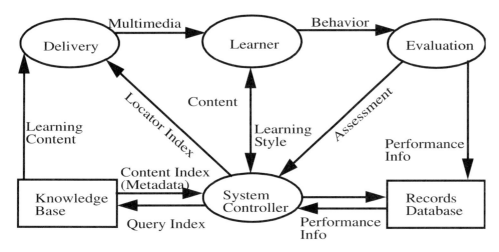

Figure 15: IEEE-LTSC-architecture

video, etc.) is available. The selection of media bricks is then determined by the preferences of each user.

The general functionality of Multibook, in other words the generation of lessons, is based on the knowledge base stored in the ConceptSpace. This approach is similar to the standardization by IEEE, as IEEE proposes the use of a knowledge library (knowledge base) which is responsible for the sequencing of a lesson, while the actual compilation of the lesson is performed by a delivery component (see Figure 15). It is essential to understand the setup of our knowledge base in order to understand the automatic creation of lessons.

The architecture of Multibook is presented in Figure 16. It should be noticed that the architecture is very similar to the one proposed by the IEEE-LTSC (Learning Technology Standards Committee) Learning Object Metadata group [FEH+00].

Considering the way an author writes a document, the following task can be specified: (1) an author acquires background knowledge, (2) an author creates an outline for a document, (3) an author fills the outline with content. These steps are modeled by different spaces in Multibook. The ConceptSpace contains an ontology in terms of keywords which is necessary to create the outline of a lesson. After the sequencing of the outline (equally to the creation of a table of contents) the actual content (text, images, audio, video, animation) is filled into the outline using elements of the second space, the MediaBrickSpace. A general abstraction of Multibook is that it is necessary to employ different relations within the ConceptSpace and the MediaBrickSpace to model the different goals which both spaces have. There are objects (concepts and media bricks), relations (semantic relations in the ConceptSpace and rhetorical-didactic relations in the MediaBrickSpace), and attributes of the media bricks. Being used as an index to the original learning material (an approach much closer to publishing practice than to ITS or expert systems, related to structuring and reusing assets etc.) the facts in the ConceptSpace will not mirror each assertion that is made in the media bricks.

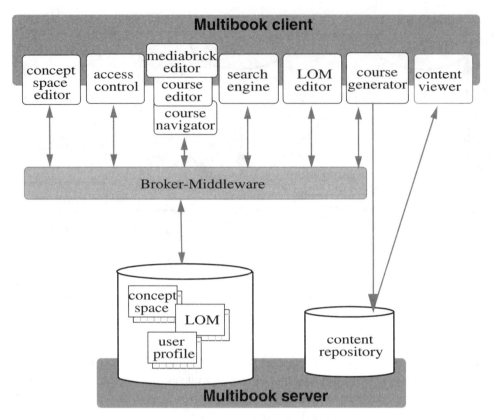

Figure 16: MultiBook architecture

4.1.2 ConceptSpace

A great advantage of the separation of concepts from content is that the content in the system can be modified or changed without affecting the overall structure stored in the ConceptSpace. It is also relatively easy to extend parts of a document, for example by deepening explanations or by examples, if additional media bricks are inserted. The process of inserting additional media bricks does not change the ConceptSpace [SSR+99c], [FEH+00], and [SRH+01].

As a rule of thumb, the level of granularity, i.e., the detail and extent to which the subject field as well as the learners' knowledge about it is modeled, is chosen to identify topics that could serve as Chapter headings in a multimedia study book.

Formally, this is realized as an entity relationship model, where each object appears only once and accumulates information. While some instance objects may be relevant (a concrete person or company, etc.), the main part of the network will be formed by abstract concepts. Such a focus on topics/concepts suggests that the ConceptSpace will be a terminological

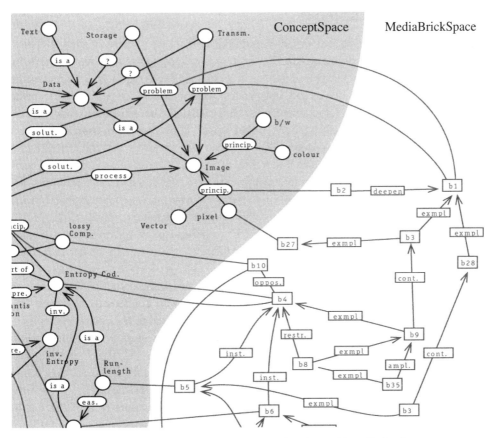

Figure 17: Part of the Multibook net for the multimedia book

ontology rather than an axiomatized ontology[2] [Sow91], i.e., an ontology whose concepts and relations have associated axioms and definitions that are stated in logic or some computer oriented language that can be automatically translated to logic.

The ConceptSpace is created and stored as an ontology, which has three constituents: concepts, relations among the concepts, and axioms. The basis of our conceptual instantiation and storage is the Smalltalk Frame Kit (denoted by SFK) developed by Rostek and Fischer at GMD-IPSI [LF]. SFK is a framework for both data modeling and procedural knowledge engineering. The last feature guarantees a continuous application of the axioms in our ontology.

---

[2]An ontology is a construction of knowledge models which specify concepts or objects, their attributes, and interrelationships.

4.1.3 MediaBrickSpace

Media bricks can either be text or other multimedia elements such as images, graphics, video, and audio streams or interactive visualizations implemented as Java applets [EFS99], [PED+99]. Individually tailored presentations of learning material require to integrate media bricks at an arbitrary point in a lesson, independent from their media type. One prerequisite for that is modularity; texts, for example, must be formulated without references to previous pieces of text. instructional visualizations should be used in different learn context, therefore should be developed as context independent modules. We are aware that the generation of modular, reusable resources requires a new way of writing or development, because generally it is not known in which environment a resource is integrated and used. With this, not only the environment of the content of the resource but also the way how it is presented is meant. Furthermore it is necessary that information about content, grade of detail, and underlying pedagogical concept of a media brick is available to the system in order to guide its decisions. A specific problem is the level of difficulty which is not a matter of a single media brick.

A coherent lesson is a lesson where the relations between the parts (media bricks) are well defined. Coherence is difficult to achieve in systems with a modular knowledge base [SSS00b]. For this purpose the media bricks are not only linked to the corresponding concept but also interconnected in the MediaBrickSpace by rhetorical-didactic relations based on the Rhetorical Structure Theory [MT87].

In general, the rules for building the lesson out of the relevant media bricks have to use the rhetorical relations and the characteristics of the media bricks, in order to match the users' level of difficulty, media preferences and coherence expectations [SSR+99b]. Simultaneously, they have to work off the structure of the lesson compiled earlier and to fulfil the demands of the users' learning method. Note that the learning method requires rules working on both spaces. These goals are not always easily harmonized: As candidates for the next media brick in a particular lesson, a brick that is connected to the current one will compete against bricks connected to the next topic in the planned structure [SSR+99a]. To be able to generate lessons according to the user's needs, the knowledge base of the systems has to provide meta-information [SSR+99c].

4.1.4 Metadata

Enabling a system to make decisions about the relevance or the order of media bricks requires more information about the media brick than just the raw content. This information has to be stored either embedded within the actual media brick or somewhere separated from the content in the knowledge base [SSFS99]. This requires a data model for describing the media bricks which can be used inside the system and is also suitable for tasks like pure information retrieval on the Web. Most of the existing web-based hypermedia learning systems use self developed models, which are only useful in the closed system, for describing their resources. This makes it very difficult for a user with no detailed knowledge about the system, to add new material to the system and link the material to already available resources. Therefore we decided to examine existing and widely used metadata approaches for describing our learning material. Such an approach has to fulfil the requirements mentioned above, especially the possibility to connect the media bricks to other media bricks and to the terms of the ontology in the ConceptSpace. Based on the studies envestigated in Chapter 3, the only sophisticated approach currently available is LOM. Using LOM, we found out that it is very suitable for static media bricks (text, images,...), but it was insufficient to use it for dynamic media bricks (interactive, adaptive visualizations) [EGFS00], [EFS01]. Dynamic metadata fields to be used within the context of Multibook are described in Section 4.2.1.

4.2 Dynamic Metadata

Multibook generates presentations and lessons out of the media bricks contained in the MediaBrickSpace, using the topics contained in the ConceptSpace. The courses to be presented are composed out of modules (static and/or dynamic). A media brick can be selected, when the system comes to the decision that it is sensible to present the user this media brick on a certain place, and that the prerequisites according to hardware, software, and transfer-capacity are met. Concerning the content aspect, it is also possible to offer only optionally

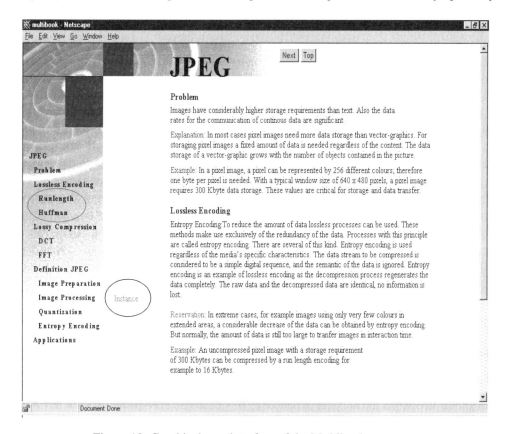

Figure 18: Graphical user interface of the Multibook prototype

media bricks to a user. Multibook realizes this option by the presentation of a media brick as "StretchText". An example can be seen in Figure 18. Here, a deepening component is not presented directly to a user but is listed by its title to the left site of the other media bricks which are shown to the user. By clicking the title, the media brick is integrated into the existing sequence. The illustration shows that this technology can be used not only for the presentation of individual media bricks but also for complete sections of the presentation.

In this example, some of the subsections of the learning unit (left hand side) are also only offered optionally. The application of "StretchText" with optional media bricks - instead of that in HTML presentations usual utilization of conventional links, which refer to a new side-helps the user to keep the context in view in which this resource is inserted. The local coherence is increased. Furthermore, the "lost in hyperspace" syndrome is weakened. The user doesn't receive a completely new side that he can leave only by clicking buttons again.

A further variant of dynamic behaviour are the dynamic media bricks used in Multibook. These media bricks are Java based, interactive simulations that can be parameterized. In accordance with the input-parameters, these media bricks can offer different means of interaction or can present the material on different variations. An example is shown in Figure 19. It is a screenshot of a Java applet describing the Discrete Cosine Transformation. The illustration shows the applet as represented to an inexperienced user. The means of interaction are restricted to the essential ones. The user has no possibilities, for example, to alter the formulas for the transformation into frequence space (in the right lower quadrant). He only has the possibility to choose this excerpt of the picture the coefficients of should be calculated. The applet is presented to a more experienced user with the same surface. But in this case, the formula can be altered directly by the user and the resulting alterations of the transformation are directly visible. This dynamic behaviour of this media brick is realized by the mapping of the content preferences and the prior knowledge of the user stored in the user profile to the corresponding parameters of the applets like for instance LOM.Educational.DifficultyLevel (see Appendix B). This way, one media brick can be used not only in different learning units, but also in various modes (see next section).

With the presentation of media bricks as optional components, the decision is up to the user whether he would like to see this media brick or not. The dynamics therefore is based on decisions that are made outside the system. Later on, these decisions of the user can have effects on decisions that the system plans autonomously. If the user chooses for example an optional media brick explaining the actual learning content in a more illustrating way, this choice can be considered by the system for the future composition of learning units, the system can add illustrating media bricks directly.

Dynamic decisions can be made also on the physical level. They can be made also within the system. Some of the decisions are based on information gained before the user starts the actual learning, and some are based on the user's action while he is learning. A dynamic adaptation during the use of the system could be for example the scaling of a video stream during the transfer, if it can be determined by quality of service control mechanisms, that a certain bandwidth can be guaranteed.

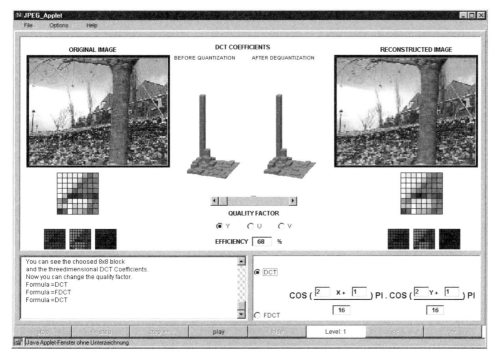

Figure 19: Dynamic media brick

The decision about the presentation format is not done by the system autonomously, but is up to the user. Multibook offers PDF and HTML as presentation schemes. Although PDF files can be read directly on the screen via corresponding viewers and multimedia components can be integrated into the document by links, the texts and pictures are normally printed out and read "off-line" by the user. Therefore, an adaptation of the learning unit to physical conditions is not necessary. In this case, the system has only the task to convert the content of the selected media bricks to the PDF format.

4.2.1 Adaptation of Visualization to User Preferences

When working with media bricks and with the necessary educational metadata, an important disadvantage becomes obvious: Due to the history of the development of metadata, primarily static resources, such as images or text documents can be described properly. Unfortunately, an appropriate description of dynamic resources, for example animations, is feasible only to a limited extent. The reason is that dynamic multimedia objects can process input parameters, generate output parameters, and also work internally with data which cannot be described in the traditional metadata schemes.

To be able to integrate dynamic metadata into an automatically generated lesson in Multibook, and to reuse this media brick in different context (req. #1) according to a desired learn situation based on the background knowledge of the user (req. #2) an appropriate practice set of metadata vocabulary was defined based on the general definition of the dynamic metadata category as an extension to the IEEE LOM. In the following we analyze the requirements of the proposed set of metadata for dynamic content in detail.

- *Language*:
  LOM contains a field to store information about the language which is used within a learning object. However, dynamic media bricks enable the user to change that language. An example is Java's internationalization framework where a set of language alternatives can be used. Although it would be possible to change the underlying LOM base category, we propose to use a new field within the new category "Dynamic Metadata" containing a list of possible languages. The original LOM field could then be used to store the initial state of a dynamic media brick.

- *DifficultyLevel*:
  Within the category "Educational", LOM contains the field "DifficultyLevel" that describes the difficulty of a LO on a scale from "Very low" to "Very high". With regard to hierarchical modularized animation chains, such a choice is inappropriate. An example is an animation visualizing the steps of JPEG for a beginner. The level of difficulty would be "very low". A more advanced user could switch to animations of the single steps of the algorithm, an expert user could even change the components of the DCT formula. To be able to describe these difficulty changes, we introduce a new dynamic field "DifficultyLevel" which indicates the degree of difficulty the resource should start with. The values should (like in the LOM base model) range from "Very low" to "Very high". Modularized hierarchical animations have for example been described in [EFS99] and [EDS00]. This field is suitable for the reusability and customizability issue required (req. #1 and req. #2).

- *InteractivityLevel*:
  The same argumentation with regard to the field "DifficultyLevel" is true for the degree of interactivity of a resource. While a beginner might use a visualization of a problem in a movie-like style, an expert might want to change parameters and thus use a highly interactive application. We propose a new field "InteractivityLevel", storing the degree of interactivity on a scale from "Very low", "Low", "Normal", "High", to "Very high".

- *Bidirectional*:
  Some animations or visualizations offer the possibility to step forward or back. We propose to use a field "Bidirectional" indicating whether a step-back operation is possible or not depending on the learn situation.

- *Dimension*:
  For some animations it is necessary to specify the dimension of the container in which the visualization will take place. This is necessary for the automatic generation of lessons. LOM provides a similar field "Physical Size" which describe the size in Bytes and not the appropriate size on the graphical user interface in pixels or dots.

- *Topic*:
  Many dynamic visualizations explain an algorithm or a behaviour. We propose to use a field "Topic" to store the name of an algorithm to be presented (visualized). Another possibility would be to extend the meaning of the field "Name" of the base LOM scheme. The disadvantage of the latter approach would be that a clear distinction between the

parts of an algorithm would be impossible. An example is a JPEG animation where the field "Name" contains the string "JPEG", while the dynamic metadata field "Algorithm" might contain the string "Entropy Encoding".

- *Scenario*:

  A scenario is a specific form of an animation which is defined by a teacher and intended to explain a subset of the knowledge an applet (dynamic media brick or instructional visualization) could transfer. Similar to the field "Topic", a dynamic media brick can be used to visualize various scenarios. An example is an applet explaining Ethernet. Possible scenarios are for example "Shortframe" or "Collision". The new field "Scenario" has a general meaning as it can be identified in visualization; it is somehow an alternative to the field "Topic". To be able to describe a scenario adequately, we define two more new fields: "Mode" and "Name". In the mode field we offer a selection of the values "Problem", "Solution", and "Guidedtour". The name field stores the name of the respective scenario. The field "Scenario" can then store choices of the things an applet can explain. The items of the lists can have a different degree of interactivity. This field has been used for instance in the parade lesson presented later in this Chapter.

- *InputData*:

  A very important new field with regard to dynamic metadata is the field "InputData". Regular static resources don't need any input data. Dynamic Learning Objects can be parameterized by input data. The same applet can then be used to animate different topics. An example use of this field are sorting algorithms. It is sometimes necessary to change the input data to investigate the differences of the diverse sorting algorithms. Input data can for example be stored in a serialized way in a file. The field "InputData" then contains the file name of the input data.

- *OutputData*:

  Like input data, a dynamic media brick can communicate with the outside world using output data which can be stored in a serialized way in a file. The field "OutputData" of the category "dynamic metadata" would then contain the name of the file.

- *Explanation*:

  Many multimedia learning objects come with some sort of explanation, for example a text motivating a problem, or an audio introduction explaining the screen setup, or the processing which is visualized in the dynamic media brick. We propose to use a new dynamic category "explanation" with the fields "Type" and "Media". The type of an explanation can for example be "Hints", "Errors", "Logs", or "Information". The type "Hints" can for example activate a hint narration of the topic to be visualized. The type "errors" could activate an error rendering of the topic to be visualized. In some cases it can be very useful to inform the user about errors which result from an incorrect use of parts of a visualization. The type "logs" can activate a narration of the logs of an applet visualizing a topic which can be used to discover the history of the use of a dynamic media brick. The type "Information" can activate an explanation of the general steps of an algorithm to be visualized. Many animations which can be found nowadays don't use an explanation of the animation itself which makes it sometimes hard to use the animation (req. #4). The field "Media" contains information about the storage format of the available explanation. Possible values are "Text", "Audio", or "Video". As an example, a combination of "Information" and "Audio" stored in the fields of the category "Explanation" would explain the functionality of the animation using a prerecorded audio file.

The general structure of the dynamic metadata category extending the base LOM scheme is shown in Table 4.

No.	Property	Description	Example
1	*Code Information*	The information concerning the code of the dynamic media brick	-
1.1	codeName	The name of the start code of the dynamic media brick	a.class, a.flash, etc.
1.2	codeLocation	Denotes where the dynamic media brick s located	URI
1.3	codePackage	The name of the package or zip of the dynamic media brick	a.jar, a.zip, etc.
2	*Presentation Information*	The information concerning how the dynamic media brick is to be presented	-
2.1	Language	The language, the dynamic media brick should start with.	en, de, fr, etc.
2.2	DifficultyLevel	The degree of difficulty the resource should start with.	very low, low, normal, high, very high
2.3	InteractivityLevel	The degree of interactivity of the resource.	very low, low, normal, high, very high
2.4	Dimension	The 3 dimensions Information of the visualization unit.	x,y,z
2.5	Bidirectional	Indicates whether the explanation, visualization can be done in the back direction or not.	yes, no
3	*Topic Information*	Information about the topic / phenomena to be visualized.	-
3.1	Topic	The name of the topic to be shown by the resource.	Fifo, Earliest Deadline First,...

Table 4: Proposed appropriate-practice fields of dynamic metadata for Multibook

3.2	Scenario	The name of the scenario to be visualized by the resource.	-
3.2.1	Mode	Intention of the teacher with regard to the dynamic media brick.	problem, solution, normal, guidedTour
3.2.2	Name	Stores the name of a scenario.	collision, shortframe
3.3	InputData	The name of the input file needed by the resource to start properly.	parameters.txt
3.4	OutputData	The name of the output file the resource should generate.	parameters.txt
4	*Explanation Information*	Indicates which kind of explanation is required for a smart learning object.	-
4.1	Type	A list of possible explanation types.	Information, warning, error, log, hint
4.2	Media	A list of possible media types to be used for the explanation	Text, audio, video

Table 4: Proposed appropriate-practice fields of dynamic metadata for Multibook

Again, it should be noted that the LOM base scheme already introduced some fields which are similar to the ones described above. An example is the field "language". These fields are however not well suited to describe the special abilities of multimedia content.

4.2.2 Enhanced Tagging Engine

A crucial point for a widespread use of metadata standards is the amount of information needed to describe learning objects. The problem with metadata information like LOM is mainly the accurateness and the amount of time a user has to invest to describe a resource. Although many of the LOM elements can be generated automatically, there is still a significant number of elements, which should be inserted by the human being responsible of the tagging process.

To facilitate the tagging process of learning resources a special metadata editor called LOM editor was developed. The editor stores static and dynamic metadata in a relational database. To access the data stored in the SQL database we developed a three tier architecture using Java Data Base Connectivity (JDBC) [SRH+00], and [SRH+01].

We also implemented a tool to customize interactive visualizations with the use of dynamic metadata. We call this tool, "content customizer". We use the content customizer to customize an interactive multimedia Learning Object in different ways for the specific purposes of a lesson. We are then able to use visualizations several times in a learning unit, according to the context of the unit. In Figure 23, an interactive multimedia Learning Object is reused within different scenarios with different metadata sets to show different aspects of the same topic.

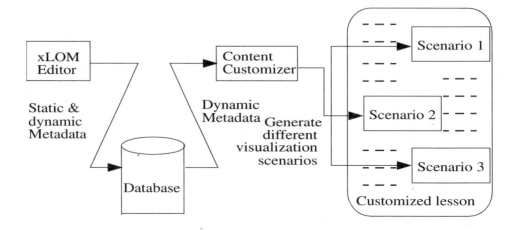

Figure 20: Instructional Visualization tagging and customization process

In the following we describe the tool which we use to create both static and dynamic metadata. The tool can also be used to publish metadata records for various resources, e.g., documents, images, audio clips, videos, animations, virtual reality worlds, or multimedia exercises.

A metadata record consists of a set of elements, describing a multimedia resource. Examples of these elements are date of creation or publication, type, author, format, or title of a resource. To access and discover multimedia information resources in a comfortable way, we developed a tool, the LOM editor, based on the IEEE-LOM scheme version 5.0. The LOM editor can be used to create and store LOM records in a relational database, and can also be used to query the database and to navigate on a resulting metadata set. We started with the development of a LOM editor due to section 3.4. We extended the LOM editor to a new editor called xLOM (Extended LOM) editor by adding an extra category for dynamic metadata, because of the recommendation of section 4.3.1.

When tagging the source material with the LOM editor, an interesting experience turned out: Most elements of a lesson to be described apply the same basic metadata information, such as the name of the author, the rights of the lesson, or the targeted user group. It would hence be very useful to use a set of templates to tag the material. Templates can avoid the necessity to fill a lot of fields again and again, for example the owner fields, the necessary browser requirements, and many more. In our current implementation, templates are used to store information, which is then only typed in once and can be applied multiple times. To be able to exchange metadata with other applications, we included an XML-based import/export functionality as part of the xLOM editor.

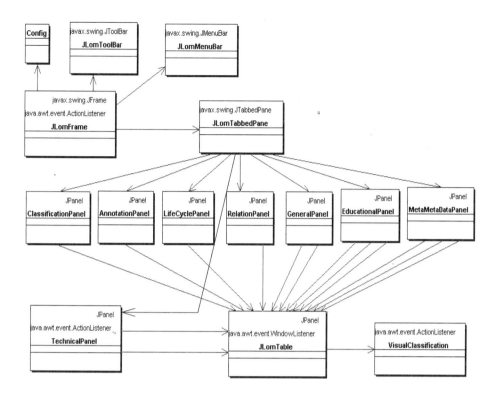

Figure 21: UML diagram of the LOM Editor

We used the xLOM editor to tag various multimedia elements, for example the Java applets that were developed as part of the Multibook project. Figure 22 shows the user interface of the xLOM editor, where most LOM categories are accessible via tabbed panes. Some of the categories (Right and Life Cycle) have been combined in order to obtain a better user interface design. Figure 22 shows the category "educational" of the LOM scheme, describing the simulation (applet) of the IIEEE-802.3 Ethernet protocol [Eth00] taken as an example and discussed later in Section 4.4.

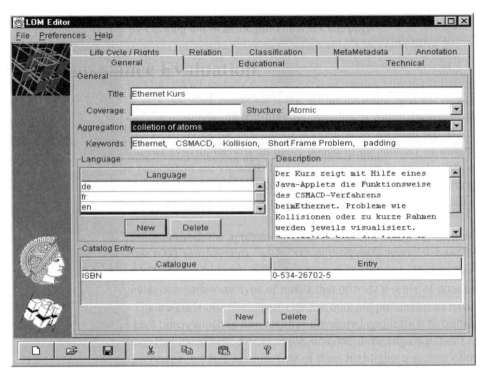

Figure 22: Graphical user interface of the xLOM - Editor

4.2.3 Enhanced Customizing Engine

The customization of interactive visualization to be used within the context of Multibook can be done automatically through the use of the Bean Markup Language [Joh99] or semi-automatic through the use of a self implemented customization engine. While the former require a knowledge in writing XML-syntax, the second has a graphical user interface.

As discussed before, dynamic metadata contain properties of multimedia learning objects, and a set of suitable values for each property. By customizing dynamic objects, exactly one of these values will be assigned to its related property. The content customizer read the metadata description stored in the database (SQL and XML-based databases are supported). The content is then displayed on the graphical user interface of the customizer as depicted in Figure 23. An interactive visualization can then be parametrized by selecting the necessary values for each parameter. The result can be stored in XML or HTML syntax.

```
...
<GENERAL>
<TITLE>
<LANGSTRING LANG= "de">Ethernet Kurs</LANGSTRING>
<LANGSTRING LANG="en">Ethernet Course</LANGSTRING>
</TITLE>
<LANGUAGE> de </LANGUAGE>
<DESCRIPTION>
<LANGSTRING LANG="de"> The functionality of Ethernet will be shown
</LANGSTRING>
</DESCRIPTION>
<KEYWORDS>
<LANGSTRING LANG="de">Ethernet</LANGSTRING>
</KEYWORDS>
</GENERAL>

<DYNAMIC>
<PARAMETER>
<PARAMETERNAME> algorithm</LANGSTRING>
<PARAMETERVALUE> non-persistent</LANGSTRING>
</PARAMETER>
<PARAMETER>
<SCENARIO>
<SCENARIONAME> problem</LANGSTRING>
<SCENARIOVALUE> collision</LANGSTRING>
</SCENARIO>
</PARAMETER>
...
</DYNAMIC>
...
```

Listing 1: Excerpt of the LOM description of the Ethernet parade lesson

An example is the dynamic metadata field "Scenario" where the content customizer allows to select a mode (for example guided tour), together with a name of a scenario which has been stored before. Listing 2 shows an excerpt of the generated HTML page for the example stored before (Listing 1).

The suitability of the component-based development of interactive visualization enhanced with the above defined dynamic metadata fields will be discussed in the next section, where a parade lesson is described and some usability studies have been done.

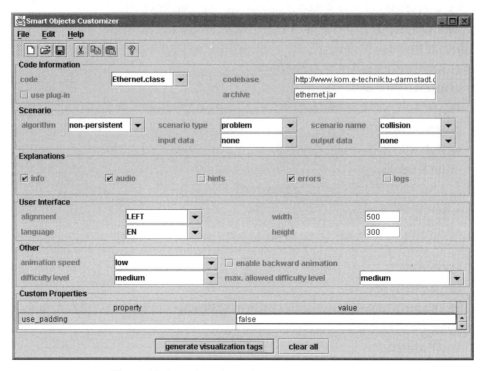

Figure 23: User interface of the content customizer

4.3 ITBeanKit: Interactive Teaching Bean Kit

The content of the prototype version of the Multibook system is based upon the printed book "Multimedia: Computing, Communications & Applications" by Ralf Steinmetz and Klara Nahrstedt [SN95] consisting of about 1000 pages, and a selection of instructional visualizations. As described above, one part of Multibook system is content development tools.

To be able to cope with alternative representations of concepts and phenomena and to allow end-users to adapt and customize already developed instructional visualizations according to their needs, as well as to facilitate developers work in creating interactive software visualizations from already developed components. We decided to implement a multimedia content development framework to simplify the development process by promoting the reuse of code, patterns, and domain expertise. This tool is called interactive Teaching Bean Kit (iTBeanKit).

```
...
<APPLET
CODE="Ethernet.class" ARCHIVE="ethernet.jar"
CODEBASE="http://www.kom.e-technik.tu-darmstadt.de/projects/iteach/itbean-
kit/applets/paradelektion/index.html"
WIDTH="500" HEIGHT="300" ALIGN="LEFT" >
<PARAM = "algorithm" VALUE = "non-persistent">
<PARAM = "scenarioName" VALUE = "problem">
<PARAM = "scenarioValue" VALUE = "collision">
<PARAM = "explanationInfo" VALUE = "true">
<PARAM = "explanationError" VALUE = "true">
<PARAM = "explanationAudio" VALUE = "true">
...
</APPLET>
...
```

Listing 2: Excerpt of a through the costemizer generated HTML page

4.3.1 Design Issues

Several ways exist to develop instructional visualizations for web-based learning systems like Multibook, among other Macromedia Flash animations, Microsoft ActiveX, and Java applets. Based on the comparison done in sction 3.2.4, we decided to use applets. Applets are content and therefore they are stored in the MediaBrickSpace. They are like all other media bricks tagged with metadata in order to find them and reuse them (req. #1). Java applets are employed very often to explain complex processes to deepen the understanding of difficult parts of educational documents [ESH+97]. However, the use of Java applets does not have to be restricted to simulations or visualizations of specific problems. Many examples show that applets can be used for exercises and tests and therefore offer more flexibility than other media [PED+99]. One advantage of using applets is the possibility to use parameters so that they can be used for different learners and preferences [EDS00] (req. #2). Their integration in different learn context, however, requires a new set of dynamic metadata.

As a result of the evaluation in section 3.2.4, the iTBeanKit is based on the JavaBeans technology [Eng97], [ON98'], [OH98], and [FE99]. Although it is currently implemented in Java, the Interactive Bean (ItBean) specification is independent of implementation language and adopted component model and technology.

The next section sets up the common environment for all the applets that will be implemented within the iTBeanKit as part of the Multibook project. Our framework contains several methods that can be used in different applications. These methods are empty and have to be filled by programmers according to the specific needs of the specific application. iTBeanKit provides the user with a work space where visualization components can be wired together. When executed, all the components are contained within windows, thereby facilitating their easy resizing, placement, and closure.

4.3.2 General-Purpose Classes

The packages kom.itbeankit.itbeanframe and kom.itbeankit.common contains all those common classes, that are used by component developers. The first package contains the classes and interfaces needed for a unified graphical user interface. The latter package consists of those methods and interfaces that are model based and will discussed first.

Every Bean in this project possess a row of common properties and functionalities. The StandardBean interface is not only important to guarantee an uniform communication between the components. In addition, It declares the properties mainly -get- and -set- Methods and the registration methods for the ItBeanCommunicationEvent. Also, the different metadata items defined in this work (Section 4.2.1) are contained in this interface as variables, with their respective get- and set- methods.

The abstract class ItBean implements the interface StandardBean and serves as superclass to all developed visualizations. Furthermore, the class ItBeanCommunicationEvents defines the events according to the description in section 3.2.5.

The construction kit (described in Section 4.3.6) as well as all other components interested in an ItBeanCommunicationEvent have to implement the interface ItBeanCommunicationListener. To distribute the fired events to the corresponding and interested listener we developed the class ItBeanEventMulticaster. Each itBean has zero or more pins (according to section 3.2.5), through which it can be linked to other components and functionally cooperate with them by exchanging data. This functionality is implemented in the ItBeanPin class. To allocate virtual space for the results of the computing of individual Beans, the collection class DataPool was implemented. ItBeanFileName fixes the "virtual" file-names for the components, under which they can either store their data on hard disk or in the DataPool.

In the following an excerpt of the StandardBean Interface is given.

```
package kom.itbeankit.common;
import java.awt.*;
public interface StandardBean
{
    //Topic Information
    //use example: setTopic(new String("Ethernet"))
    static final String TOPIC = "theTopic";
    static final String SCENARIO = "theScnario";

    ...
}
```

Listing 3: Excerpt of the StandardBean Interface

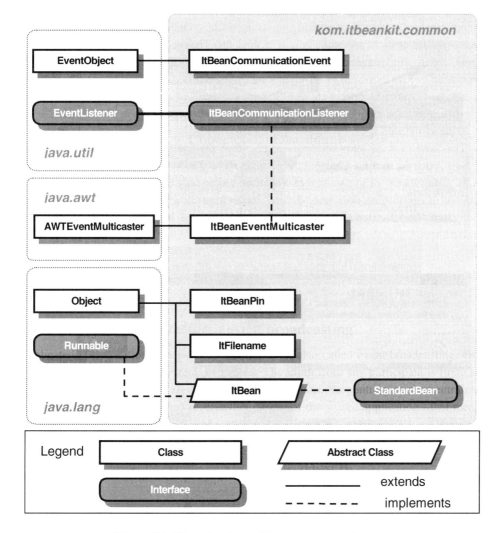

Figure 24: Class structure of the common package

4.3.3 Graphical User Interface

The model-view-controller (MVC)-model (see section 3.1.4) adapted to the component-based development is used to generate itBeans. This model is also responsible for a unified environment of the itBeans, which do not have to care about the graphical presentation of their input and output.

To have a unified interaction model and thus to simplify the usage of the applets (req. #4), two main parts of the graphical user interface can be identified (see Figure 25): The first is the unified control unit, formed by a menu placed at the top of the screen and a ControButtonPanel (VCR-like) placed at the bottom. This unified control unit is common for all applets. The VCR is in charge of steering the progression of the explanation, while the menu executes general actions like opening or saving a file, changing the language or the appearance of the frame up to providing help if wished, etc. The second part is built up by three different areas. The bigger one named "MainPanel" for illustrating the animation. The "TextArea" where messages of different kind (hints, errors,...) explaining the behavior of the topic to be visualized, appears and the "ParameterPanel", in which diverse parameters of the current explanation can be changed. The size of the panels can be modified, giving flexibility to the visualization.

The separation of texts and parameters from the main explanation seemed sensible because, once the user has changed the parameters he wants, he can concentrate his attention on the "MainPanel" or in a written explanation, seeing only things related to the explanation and not things that he does not need to concentrate on any more, like already changed parameters. This division of the graphical user interface has been proven to be very useful as students reported in the evaluation described in Section 4.4.4.

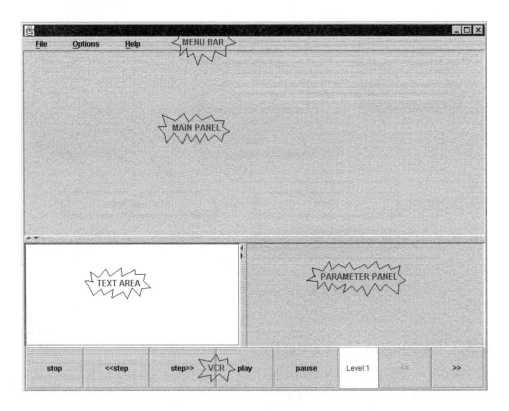

Figure 25: Graphical user interface of itBeanFrame

4.3.4 User Interaction

To simplify the usage of the interactive visualizations (applets), a common components "ControlButtonPanel" has been developed. This component also named VCR is responsible for the invocation of the proper method call corresponding to an event. The VCR is built up by seven buttons to control the course of the explanation. Each button performs the action indicated by its name. They can also be disabled in case they are not necessary.

Figure 26: ControlButtonPanel (VCR)

Our ControlButtonPanel currently reacts on the following events: start, stop, pause, next, previous, level down, and level up. To simplify the interaction with the user interface only those buttons are highlighted which are applicable. Using the components at the lowest level of the hierarchy, i.e., only the level up-button is highlighted.

ID	Called methods	Explanation
PLAY	play (ActionEvent e)	This method is invoked if the play button sources an ActionEvent
STOP	stop (ActionEvent e)	This method is invoked if the stop button sources an ActionEvent
PAUSE	pause (ActionEvent e)	This method is invoked if the pause button sources an ActionEvent
FORWARDS	forwards (ActionEvent e)	This method is invoked if the forwards button sources an ActionEvent
BACKWARDS	backwards (ActionEvent e)	This method is invoked if the backwards button sources an ActionEvent
LEVELUP	levelUp (ActionEvent e)	This method is invoked if the level up button sources an ActionEvent
LEVELDOWN	levelDown (ActionEvent e)	This method is invoked if the level down button sources an ActionEvent

Table 5: ItBeanControlEvents and the corresponding ItBeanControlListeners methods

The class ControlButtonPanel contains an inner class which implements java.awt.event.ActionListener and extends the standard action-IDs as of Java to the IDs presented in Table 5. These events are generated, when a click on the GUI of the VCR occurred. The explanation accompanying each instructional visualization contains three items:

- Errors: indicates whether error messages should be given and appear in the Text area or not
- Hints: if selected, hints about next interaction will be displayed in the Text area
- Audio: if selected, audio files will be played during the explanation

to achieve learn effectivity we give the possibility to integrate text, animation, audio, and interaction in the explanation. We take for especially effective the introduction of the audio because it allows to concentrate on the animation while hearing the explanation simultaneously. The explanation can also be displayed in the text area giving the chance to read it up. Text as well as audio explanations support internationalization as described next.

4.3.5 Internationalization Support

Information technology, by influencing the ways we live and work, learn about the world, and interact with each other, is having profound effects on the global society and economy. Developing software for different cultures is hard to achieve. Internationalization of software is a complex topic because the world counts so many permutations of cultures and languages. Research on technologies and systems facilitating multilingual information access, retrieval, extraction, translation, and summarization is still in the early stage [LJTD95], [Hof95]. None the less, efforts on internationalization of interfaces and technologies for the localization of on-line multimedia content for handling cultural diversity exist [SM99]. Most of the time, internationalization support, however, is restricted to text. Adapting the layout (graphical user interface) to specific culture needs are less considered. It should be noted that the presentation of the content itself (i.e., through an image) depends strongly on the culture it is made for.

To support different culture group, internationalization in this work is not only supported through textual explanation as mentioned above, but also through changing the direction of the visualization window (Layout). This is done in the centerPanel Bean, which contain the three Panels described above "MainPanel", "ParameterPanel", and "TextArea".

The methods chageOrientation(), chageOrientationHorizontal(), and chageOrientation-Vertical() are responsible for changing the Layout according to the desired culture group. In the Latin speaking world, where words are written from the left to the right, it is appropriate to have a wider space for the explanation area (TextArea) than for instance in the Chinese speaking world. In the Chinese culture, it is preferred to elongate the explanation area, because Chinese is written from the top to the bottom.

```
...
public void changeOrientation() {
storeOrientation = splitPane.getOrientation();
splitPane.setOrientation(splitPaneBottom.getOrientation());
splitPaneBottom.setOrientation(storeOrientation);
}
public void changeOrientationVertical() {
splitPane.setOrientation(JSplitPane.VERTICAL_SPLIT);
splitPaneBottom.setOrientation(JSplitPane.HORIZONTAL_SPLIT);
}
public void changeOrientationHorizontal() {
splitPane.setOrientation(JSplitPane.HORIZONTAL_SPLIT);
splitPaneBottom.setOrientation(JSplitPane.VERTICAL_SPLIT);
}
...
```

Listing 4: Internationalization support on the GUI

4.3.6 Construction Kit

To support the constructivist learning theory [Kos96], iTBeanKit provides the user with a work space where visualization components can be introduced, linked, and where interaction can take place. When executed, all the components are contained within windows, thereby facilitating their easy resizing, placement, and closure. An important aspect in our framework is substitution, which means that an end-user can exchange an ItBean with another. In the context of JPEG the exchange of discrete cosine transformation (DCT) with fast fourier transformation (FFT) may be an appropriate substitution. In the JavaBeans [jav00] component model, like many others, components interoperate by being "wired together". Wires provide a path along which data can flow. Conventional design tools, such as Symantec's VisualCafe or Borland's JBuilder allow users to connect almost any component to any other component, and require that every connection be made manually by the end user. Several techniques can be used to handle the complexity of wiring components. Each of them gives components the ability to dynamically describe their current data manipulation and connectivity capabilities:

- Java InfoBus:
  InfoBus [Jav] allows a set of data producers to broadcast the dynamic availability of data by either name or type, and allows a set of data consumers to search for by name or type. Furthermore, InfoBus mediates the process of acquiring references to data channels and releasing them when no longer needed.
- JavaBeans Reflection:
  JavaBeans provides a reflection mechanism, which can be used by design tools to dis-

cover the wiring design pattern of a given JavaBeans component. The reflection mechanism, however, does not cope well with components that dynamically change because the reflection mechanism uses a static analysis of the methods that a class implements to determine its capabilities [FE99].

- Proprietary Mechanism:

    To reduce the cognitive difficulty to designers, a proprietary mechanism was designed that dynamically handles component connection capabilities and mediates the process of establishing connections between components that have compatible capabilities, as described in section 3.2.5.

The combination of itBeans can be accomplished in two different ways: itBeans can be combined using a visual builder tool or a script specifying the components and their respective order in order to create an applet dynamically. Figure 27 shows the prototype of the iTBeanKit visual builder tool, which allows a simple wiring of the components to be tested. A detailed explanation of its functionalities can be found in [EFS99] and [ESS+99].

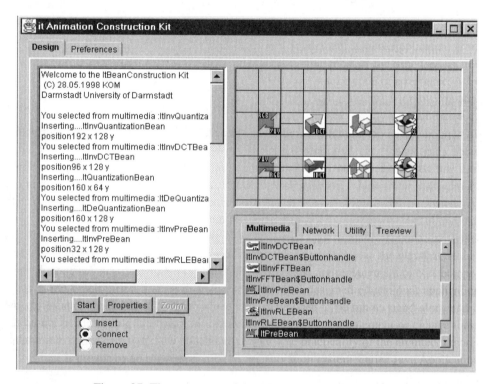

Figure 27: The prototype of the ItBean visual builder tool

The iTBeanKit provides the means for creating, editing component properties, defining and specifying the order of the events, and saving and restoring the states of itBeans. Finally the iTBeanKit manages the sequencing of the itBeans components so that they perform the intended functions. Figure 27 illustrate the graphical user interface of the construction kit developed within this work. It shows the connection of the different parts of the JPEG compression technique. The JPEG example is described in more details in Appendix B1.

4.4 Putting it All Together: Visualization of Ethernet

As an application example of the theory described in Chapter 3 and based on the iTBeanKit explained above, we developed a lesson explaining the IEEE 802.3 CSMA/CD Ethernet protocol [Eth00]. The main goal of the lesson is to demonstrate the reusability issue during the development stage (req. #1) and the possibilities that the parametrization of an animation offers. A version of the lesson can be found on the web [Mul00] or on the enclosed CD. The lesson provides an interactive environment that elicits active student participation using a carefully orchestrated presentation of information in various media, such as text, visualization, static diagrams, and interactive simulations with appropriate temporal, spatial, and hyperlink connections. User evaluation will be also presented at the end of this section.

4.4.1 Decomposition

Ethernet technology predates the Institute of Electrical and Electronics Engineers (IEEE) LAN standards committee. Therefore, the first Ethernet standard was developed by a vendor consortium made up of Digital Equipment Corp. (DEC), Intel, and Xerox. Taking the first initial of each company, the first Ethernet standard became known as the DIX Standard. This was the first open standard for LAN technology ever published.

Two versions of the DIX standard were proposed and the IEEE 802 committee made the creating of open standards for LANs one's job. The first "Ethernet-like" IEEE standard was published in 1985 and formally called the "IEEE 802.3 Carrier Sense Multiple Access with Collision Detection (CSMA/CD) Access Method and Physical Layer" specifications. The Ethernet system consists of three basic elements:

- The physical media used to carry Ethernet signals between computers.
- A set of media access control rules embedded in each Ethernet interface that allow multiple computers to access the shared Ethernet channel.
- An Ethernet frame that consists of a standardized set of fields used to carry data over the system.

Ethernet uses a bus topology, which is a networking architecture that is linear, usually by using one or more pieces of cable (Bus Element) to form a single line (Bus Segment), or bus. The signals (Signal) sent by one station (Host) extend the length of this cable to be heard by other stations. Taking this into account together with the explanations of the previous section and doing a first level decomposition of the IEEE 802.3 (CSMA/CD) Protocol according to the method described in Chapter 3, the components described in Table 6 can be identified.

Each of these components (described in Table 6) has been developed as a JavaBean following the design and implementation principles described earlier in this Chapter (Section 4.3). These components are the basic elements to implement an applet visualizing the diverse functionality of Ethernet. Figure 28 depict a screenshot of the ethernet applet developed with the above mentioned components. As seen in this figure, the visualization window is divided into three main areas according to the iTBeanKit:

- the "MainPanel", where the hosts are connected to the bus and the animation takes place
- the "ParameterPanel", where some of the interaction parameters can be adjusted, and
- the "TextArea" where the textual explanation of the animation can be drawn, in order to facilitate the understanding.

Component	Symbol	Description
Host		Represent a computer that access the shared Ethernet channel.
Arrow		Represent the data flow within a host. A sender is represented through a down directed arrow, while a receiver is represented through a up directed arrow.
Bus Element		Represent the smallest entity of the ethernet channel.
Signal		Represent the state of the ethernet channel. Blue means normal transmission, red means a collision, while yellow means padding.
Bus Segment		Is composed out of several bus elements. Each bus segment has four I/O possibilities: top, bottom, left, and right. A bus segment is traversed by the signal.

Table 6: Components of the Ethernet applet

In addition to these three panel, the VCR, and the menu can be seen. In the VCR we notice two disabled buttons, which means that the interaction with them is not possible. This is either because the functionality is not implemented, or it does not make sense to use this buttons in the context, within which the applet is integrated.

To prove the suitability of the theory described in Chapters 3 and 4, concerning the reusability requirement (req. #1), the same basic elements were used for the implementation of the applet visualizing the functionality of a Hub.

A Hub is a central device that connects stations following a star topology as an architecture. Signals sent by a station must pass through (and are usually regenerated by) these central Hubs. Since all stations are linked through the Hub, the architecture resembles a star. Figure 29 shows a screenshot of an interactive applet visualizing the functionality of a Hub.

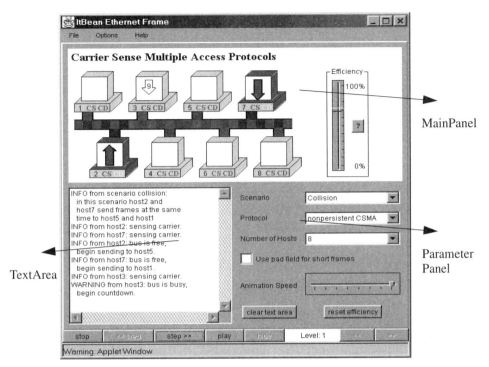

Figure 28: The Ethernet applet built up from the different components

The only difference to the Ethernet applet described above, from the software engineering and reusability point of view was the controller unit, which implemented the logical structure that connect the diverse components.

As an alternative to the Hub, Switch is an option to be taken into account. It optimizes connections with the whole bandwidth for all hosts. Its installation causes no big trouble as one has only to take the cables out of the old Hub and install them instead in the Switch. One has to take also the fact in consideration that Hubs are far less expensive than Switches are. The data transmission between two hosts generates traffic only in it's correspondent segment and not in the whole channel. Bandwidth is not shared, so every single host has 100% bandwidth towards the Switch.

From the functionality point of view, a Switch can be seen as a learning Hub. As soon as a Switch receives a data package it learns the direction of the source host from which the data package came. The data packages wanted to be sent next time to that host will be directed to the port of the host, which the Switch learned from the previous data received. We find out that a Switch operates as a Hub when it has no information. We may also say that a Hub is a non intelligent Switch. This memory has an "ageing time".

Figure 30 shows a screenshot of the applet visualizing the Switch functionality. Again from the software engineering development point of view the control unit necessary to implement the logical functionality of the Switch was different. It is also responsible for the connectivity of the components. Some new components were additionally needed, among others the ageing time component presented in the applet as a table.

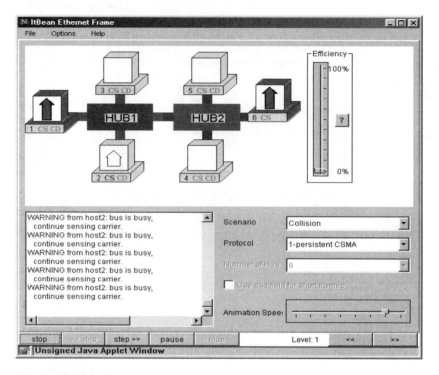

Figure 29: The Hub applet built up with the same components as Ethernet

The development of these examples was to prove the reusability issue required from the presented work. Next, a software metric is given, which present a way to measure software reusability.

4.4.2 Reusability Measurement

The phrase "We can't manage what we can't measure" holds true for the software engineering discipline. According to Poulin [Pou97] software metrics can be used to estimate costs, costs saving, and the value of software practices.

Several ways exist to determine the reusability level of a software system. One method proposed by Childs and Sametinger [CS96] determines the ratio of number of identical lines over the total number of lines. This method is appropriate for the reuse measurement based on lines and words for low-level determination of white-box frameworks (section 3.1.5).

The Software Productivity Metrics Working Group of the IEEE [BKZ93] as well as [Sam97] propose to determine the ratio of the number of reused components to the total number of components of the system, as a metric to measure software reuse. Their suggestion is presented in the following Formula.

$$\text{Reuse Level} = \frac{\text{Number of Reused Components}}{\text{Total Number of Components}}$$

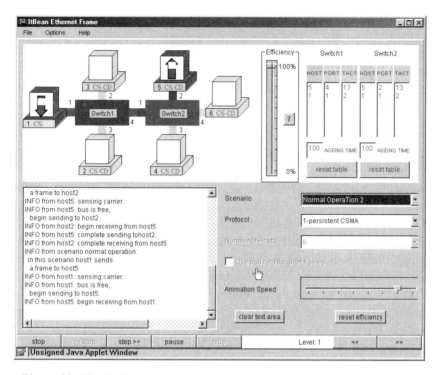

Figure 30: The Switch applet built up with the same components as Ethernet

To develop the Ethernet applet and according to the decomposition described above (Table 6), the following components (Beans) have been implemented: Signal, Arrow, BusElement, BusSegment, Host, and ItBeanEthernetFrame, as the controller (contained the logical part of the functionality of IEEE-CSMA/CD) responsible for the communication of the diverse components. These Elements were developed from scratch. In addition to these components some widgets, already developed by software vendors were used.

In addition to the first five components mentioned and developed above, the GUI components described in Section 4.3.3, and the widget components used for the parametrization (presented in the "ParameterPanel"), four more components (Beans) were necessary to visualize the functionality of a Hub. Thus a reuse level of 0.809 (17 reused components / 21 components) has been achieved.

To develop an interactive applet visualizing the functionality of a Switch, five more Beans were needed, in addition to those needed for the visualization of Ethernet. The reuse level in this situation was 0.773 (17 reused components / 22 components).

Other important aspects for measuring reusability were not considered, either because they are hard to measure like "Reuser Experience" or is subject to the evaluater, like in example "Program Documentation" [PD89].

Even if these numbers are objective, it is expedient to mention our experience during the development of these visualizations. Indeed, the Ethernet applet, had been developed by a group of two persons during a specific course (Projektseminar) at Darmstadt University of

Technology. Both the Hub applet and the Switch applet had been developed together, by another group within the scope of a similar course, 6 months later. The objective conclusion is that, even though the first group was more experienced in developing software, they needed more time in developing one applet than the second group, who needed less time in developing two applets, while reusing already developed components. According to this observation, the reusability requirement (req. #2) is maintained not only theoretically but also practically when developing instructional software corresponding to the iTBeanKit.

4.4.3 Parade Lesson

The lesson is implemented in HTML 4.0 and contains visualizations developed according to the iTBeanKit framework enhanced with the dynamic metadata set described above (Section 4.3). The lesson consists of 15 pages.

In the lesson the functionality of Ethernet is explained first. After that the student has to answer the question which problems have to be faced in a bus-topology. We provide a set of different answers and use the same animation to explain why the answers are correct or wrong. The difference between the answers is explained by different parametrization of the same animation. These parametrizations are stored as dynamic metadata for interactive visualizations as explained above. An example is shown in Figure 32 (a) where the possible answer to the question "Why is the protocol complex" is "The protocol is complex because

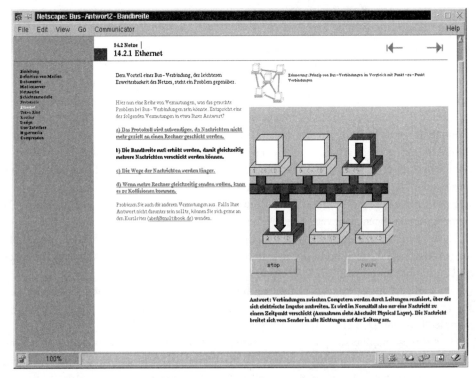

Figure 31: Screenshot of example lesson

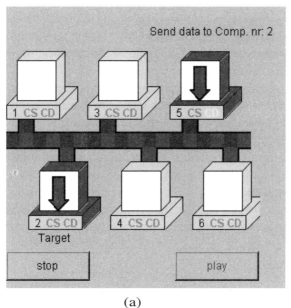

(a)

(b)

Figure 32: Examples of parametrization of dynamic media brick

messages cannot be sent to a specific computer, they can only be sent to several computers at once."

Another scenario of the same animation can also be used to provide an answer to the question "How can the collision problem be solved in Ethernet" if dynamic metadata are used. A possible answer to the question would be "Collisions cannot be avoided. If a collision is detected the transmission has to be repeated". If a collision occurs, the transmitting station recognizes the interference on the network and transmits a bit sequence called jam. The jam helps to ensure that the other transmitting station recognizes that a collision has occurred. After a random delay, the stations attempt to retransmit the information and the process begins again.

A parametrized version of the same animation used in Figure 32 (a) is illustrated in the same figure to the right (b). Note that due to the use of dynamic metadata the same animation is reused in a different context. A screenshot of the lesson is shown in Figure 31.

The lesson ends with the possibility to have an interactive simulation of the Ethernet algorithm (the Ethernet applet described above). The simulation consists of three levels. In level 1 only one out of two scenarios can be chosen (normal operation and collision problem). In level 2 more scenarios can be chosen, while in Level 3 students can build their own scenarios. In the next section the user acceptance as well as an evaluation whether the dynamic metadata affect negatively the learn process will be investigated.

4.4.4 User Evaluation

32 graduate students from Darmstadt University of Technology conducted an experiment. All of them had the possibility to interact with the lesson over the web [par00] or on the CD which accompanied the Multimedia Book written by Prof. Steinmetz [Ste00]. The questions were composed in coordination with cognitive scientists from the Department of Psychology Cognitive Science at Justus-Liebig University of Giessen [Glo].

The web-based system (EVALIS [SS01]), used for the purpose of the evaluation, is a project of the research group "instruction & interactive media" (iim) at the university Giessen. Goal of the EVALIS project is to evaluate the quality of both Internet and Intranet interactive learning systems.

One goal of that study was to prove the ideas of developing component-based visualization accompanied with metadata. The development of the lesson was to prove that through the use of dynamic metadata proposed in this work, an adaptation of the visualization according to the learn situation can be achieved (req. #2) without harming the usability issue (req. #4). In the evaluated lesson the Ethernet visualization was reused 8 times (req. #1) with different parameters, illustrating different scenarios and phenomena. Interoperability and platform independency (req. #3) of the lesson were ensured through the use of HTML and Java.

According to these goals, the questions were categorized in two group. The first were multiple choice questions and the second were "fill text" questions. The first group of questions serves to prove the theory of this work, while the second conduces the advantages and/or disadvantages of the theory respectively.

4.4.4.1 User Acceptance

The first question was about the user acceptance. All the interviewee, in generally, enjoyed working with the system. They found the multimedia elements, interesting and helpful to understand the complex procedures of Ethernet.

"fully apply" [========] 38%
"apply" [==========] 59%
"does not apply" □ 3%
"does not apply at all" | 0%

Table 7: Enjoying the work with the visualizations

Both the subjective assessment and the behaviour data speak on behalf of an acceptance of the applets. Only one person said that it has rather been for her/him no fun to look at the visualizations. All other estimations were positive (Table 7).

As seen in Table 8 only one person has looked at less than half of the visualizations. The predominant majority (84%) has looked at most or even all visualizations.

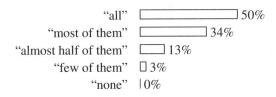

"all" [========] 50%
"most of them" [=======] 34%
"almost half of them" [==] 13%
"few of them" □ 3%
"none" | 0%

Table 8: Number of the visualizations that have been worked with

Since the content of the simulation was already clarified by the visualizations, it is difficult to draw out conclusions of the behavior data on the acceptance. It is clear however, that the predominant majority (78%) has looked at the simulation (full interactive applet) not only shortly but has come until Level2 at most. On the other hand only one fourth of the persons has scooped all possibilities of the simulation (Table 9).

"in Level 3 I defined my own Scenarios" [=====] 25%
"I tried it till Level 2" [=========] 53%
"I worked only with Level 1" [===] 13%
"I did not worked with the simulation" [==] 9%

Table 9: Intensive work with the simulation

4.4.4.2 Usability vs. Reusability

The applets consist of parametrized modules. Different but similarly looking applets can be produced from the same dynamic media brick with comparatively little expenditure as discussed in Section 4.2.1.

The predominant majority (82%) of the students gave a negative answer for the question whether the visualizations would have bored her/him. Therefore the similarity of the applets seems to be not experienced as a disadvantage. However, six persons still judge visualization as rather monotonous and another person seems to have no joy (fun) viewing visualizations (Table 10). We note that there is only a small number of students who criticize particularly the similarity of the visualizations.

"fully apply" ☐ 3%
"apply" ☐ 16%
"does not apply" ☐ 63%
"does not apply at all" ☐ 19%

Table 10: The similarity of the visualizations is monotonous and tediously

As a result we notice that the customizability of the applet to use and reuse it in different context with dynamic metadata did not experience as negative. Thus the usability (req. #4) does not suffer from the reusability.

4.4.4.3 Use Context of the Visualizations

Another interesting aspect, which does not necessarily cope with the technique described in this work, but generally, very important for research dealing with educational systems in general and instructional visualizations in particular, concerns the goals which are to be pursued with the visualizations as well as the advantages and their use.

"fully apply" ☐ 44%
"apply" ☐ 44%
"does not apply" ☐ 9%
"does not apply at all" ☐ 3%

Table 11: The Visualizations helped to better understand the functionality of Ethernet

The visualizations were considered predominantly (88%) as conducive for a better and faster understanding (Table 11). However, as seen in Table 12, they are not imperatively judged as absolutely necessary in order to understand the lessons (75%), a result which is less than

"fully apply" ☐ 6%
"apply" ☐ 19%
"does not apply" ☐ 59%
"does not apply at all" ☐ 16%

Table 12: The Visualizations would not have been needed in order to better understand the functionality of Ethernet

88%. One can still add that the majority (94%) of the students agree that there was not unnecessary loss of time through the use of visualizations (Table 13).

"fully apply" | 0%
"apply" ☐ 6%
"does not apply" ☐ 44%
"does not apply at all" ☐ 50%

Table 13: The contemplation of the visualizations costed me unnecessarily much time

Table 14 gives us an insight of when to use instructional visualizations as well as which concrete aims are to be pursued. Credence to self-study (no participation in the held lecture) was given by most of the students on an average of 82%, followed by the preparation and/or postprocessing of the lecture with an average of 71%. Using such learning presentation for the preparation of the exams has been mentioned by about half of the persons (54%).

	degree of utilization
"self study"	82%
"preparation and/or postprocessing of the lecture"	71%
"preparation of the exams"	54,33%
"As general knowledge-sources"	58,33%
"no utilization at all"	0%

Table 14: Using instructional visualization in different learn situations

Having a closer look at the learning activity (see Table 15), we note that this pattern can be broken down further. Here, first acquisition of knowledge comes up with approximately 64%, deepening of knowledge with about 61%, and repetition of knowledge comes up with 71% as the most frequently used activity. It seems that procure an overview (48%) about a specific topic as well as, well directed information searching (35%) are not the real aim of using instructional visualizations.

	degree of utilization
"first-acquisition of knowledge"	63,67%
"deepening of knowledge"	60,67%
"repeating and freshening knowledge"	71,00%
"well directed information"	35,33%
"procure an overview"	48,00%
"no utilization at all"	0 %

Table 15: Using instructional visualization for different learn activity

4.4.4.4 Conclusions

The development of the parade lesson was to prove the reusability requirement (req. #1) we addressed in this work. From the implementation point of view, we took a dynamic multimedia element (the Ethernet applet), customized it several times, and integrated it within the lesson in the appropriate context (req. #2). This form of reusability was proven to be not only possible but also user friendly (req. #4). It does not affect the user in the sense that it does not bored him.

The strength of instructional visualization integrated in the appropriate learning environment seems to lie after assessment of the interviewee in the autonomous and continuous knowledge-acquisition and refresh processes. Although the utilization is declared to the repetition and deepening of knowledge, a preparation for the exam is pulled clearly less in consideration with this learn media.

Nevertheless, the advantages of the two presentation forms clearly become evident in this realization of the parade-lesson: In a didactically planned instruction-process, the visualizations help to clarify particular, fixed courses. The simulation in the contrary enables the user to enforce individually controlled learn activities. The degree of interactivity achieved through the use of the simulation, makes it possible to discover new knowledge.

4.5 Summary

In this Chapter, an overview of Multibook was given, followed by a brief description of its architecture. The implementation of iTBeanKit, a metadata-based component-oriented framework for the development of interactive visualizations according to the theory discussed in Chapter 3 was also presented in this Chapter. Having explained the necessary category of dynamic metadata, we described our implementation of the tools which can be used for tagging, storing, and customizing dynamic media bricks. As a prototype, we implemented visualization artifacts dealing with the network protocol family "Ethernet". This prototype underwent evaluation studies dealing with reusability (req. #1), customizability (req. #2) of instructional visualization as well as their usability (req. #4), and platform independence (req. #3).

The lesson to be learned here is that thinking in images involves a different part of human consciousness from understanding mathematical symbols. A necessary component when presenting abstract ideas remains the use of text. The ideal algorithm explanation may be some sort of interactive combination of text, sound, speech, and animation. In other words, a hypertext multimedia system. These results can be taken systematically with the further development into account.

Chapter 5 Collaborative Use of Instructional Visualizations

Interactive multimedia is becoming an indispensable tool in many organizations. It is used to support many kinds of knowledge work: information retrieval, decision-making, data mining, exploration, and browsing of information spaces. However, current instructional visualization tools are limited in that they are designed to be used by only one person at a time. This restriction ignores the fact that knowledge work in most organizations is carried out by teams that may be distributed across buildings or countries. When a visualization is used in a group task, it becomes a shared artifact that will be used to assist the group's communication and coordination: in fact, visualizations' most basic tenet that "a picture is worth a thousand words" implicitly assumes that one person is attempting to communicate with another. Current visualization tools do not consider group work, and so the shared use of visualizations is made clumsy and difficult. The aim of this research is to investigate techniques for making visualizations group-aware resources. In particular, we are looking at two activities that are central to sharing instructional visualizations: Reuse stand-alone application in a shared environment (req. #5) and sharing diverse views of the same data in a managed collaborative session (req. #6).

The rest of the Chapter is organized as follows. After describing some basics for collaboration systems, some of today's state of the art collaborative tools will be discussed. followed by a presentation of the system architecture of a transparent collaborative tool ensuring our requirements (req. #5 and req. #6). Performance evaluation are then discussed.

5.1 Web-based Learning

There has been a lot of interest for Web-based tools for telelearning. One can use e-mail, newsgroup, chat rooms, and other tools which are readily available. But for efficient resource sharing one needs tools specifically designed for such purpose. These tools can be used to share educational resources and they can generally be categorized into two groups: synchronous tools and asynchronous tools. Synchronous tools are those that allow sharing of resources in real-time, such as [CGJ+98], [AWFKK97], [EKFS99], and [KFS98] and require users to be on-line at the same time. Asynchronous tools, such as Virtual U. [BSSS97], allow for mostly off-line communication and sharing. Notice that these two methods are complementary technologies, not necessarily competing. Some researchers mistakenly choose to adopt only one method, but in fact both synchronous and asynchronous resource sharing are needed for a complete system [SHE00]. As discussed in Chapter 3 Multibook is asynchronous. This is why we will focus our research now on the synchronous type. With this in mind, let us have a look at some basics about synchronous sharing.

5.1.1 Fundamentals of Real-Time Sharing

Basically speaking, the core technology behind any collaboration tool is a mechanism to enable a user to send updates to other users about the interactions that are made to a shared application, as illustrated in Figure 33. For example, when one user draws a line on a whiteboard, the system informs the whiteboards of other users so that they also draw the same line. The mechanisms to propagate these "updates" vary according to the design or intended use of the system. Some systems send graphical display updates of the portion of the screen that was changed; the receiver simply redraws that portion using the graphics update. Some other systems send the system's graphical events that were generated as a result of a user's interaction, the receivers then process the events as if generated locally; hence reproducing the interaction at every user [BSSS97], [ESGS00], and [EKFS99]. Another approach is the use of object tokens, whereby an update message is preceded by a token that defines the semantic of that update message. By looking at the token, the receivers can determine what action to perform; for example draw a line, erase an area, etc. [SG97].

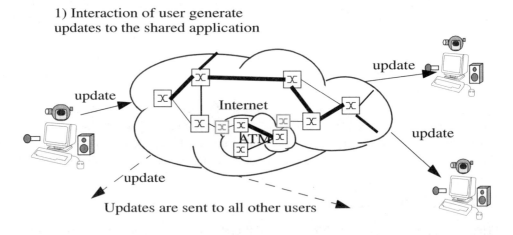

Figure 33: A generic collaboration system

All of these approaches can be implemented using a centralized or distributed communication infrastructure. Furthermore, they can be implemented as real-time or near-real-time systems. However, they all have one thing in common: they all must use reliable communication, such as TCP, for their update messages. Although suitable for real-time video/audio data transfer, unreliable communication such as UDP or regular multicasting is not suitable for the transfer of application update messages since these applications, by nature, cannot afford to lose any update data.

To optimize the use of bandwidth and compensate for latency, an approach that sends as small amount of information as possible for the updates is to be chosen. Graphics updates are therefore not suitable because of their bulkiness and heavy use of bandwidth. Event updates and object tokens are better candidates. Object tokens are heavily based on the specific application, and must in fact be hard-coded into the shared application. This is a non-transparent approach. This implicates the use of Event updates, which are what is used in our approach.

5.1.2 Synchronous Collaboration Approaches

There are two general approaches to providing computer support for synchronous collaboration. The first, collaboration awareness, includes applications specifically designed to support cooperative work. The second category is referred to as collaboration transparency based on single-user applications used in a collaborative environment.

5.1.2.1 Collaboration awareness

A collaboration-aware application is one that was developed with the aim of allowing multiple users to work cooperatively. Developing such an application has requirements beyond those of single-user applications because the programmers have to consider the interactions between the participants. Therefore the development costs are higher compared with single-user applications.

These applications may be developed ad-hoc or with a groupware toolkit. The goal of groupware toolkits is to facilitate the development of collaboration-aware applications so that they are only slightly more difficult to develop than otherwise functionally equivalent single-user applications. Nevertheless, the application programmers must explicitly build in collaboration through calls to the toolkit support functions. Therefore, whether employing a groupware toolkit or not, a collaborative-software developer must make some additional effort over that of developing an otherwise functionally equivalent single-user application. Some implementations of collaboration-aware applications are surveyed in Section 5.2, for example the Java Collaboration Environment (JCE) [AWFKK97].

5.1.2.2 Collaboration transparency

This other way of providing a synchronous collaboration is the sharing of legacy single-user applications. This is referred to as collaboration transparency, because the sharing is done by a mechanism that is unknown, or transparent, to the application and its developers. The collaboration between the participants is provided by the collaboration-tool, which modifies the application's run-time environment. So in this approach the collaboration-transparency system itself is collaboration-aware, but the single-user application is collaboration-unaware.

Several collaboration-transparency systems exist, particularly for the X Window System, for example Hewlett Packard's SharedX [GWY94]. Recently, Microsoft has released Net-

Meeting [MC99], a freely available collaboration-transparency system for the Windows platform. These collaboration systems will be discussed in more details in Section 5.2.

5.1.2.3 Awareness versus transparency

The primary benefit of collaboration-transparency systems is that, by supporting the shared use of such legacy applications, developers make no extra effort for their applications to be shared.

However, there are differences in the quality of support for collaboration that these types of systems provide. A fundamental difference is in the type of tasks they support. Collaboration-transparency systems primarily support tasks that extend from individual to collaborative performance, such as text editing. Collaboration-aware applications can also support inherently collaborative tasks, such as group decision-making. Moreover, in conventional collaboration-transparency systems all participants see exactly the same view at the same time, because the centralized application sends the same display information to all participants. This strict WYSIWIS (What You See Is What I See) may be not well suited to some applications.

When a sufficiently powerful single-user application is available to support a task, however, it makes sense to consider collaboration transparency given the lower development cost of collaboration transparency.

5.1.3 Distributed System Architectures

This section describes the feasible distributed system architectures, either centralized, where the shared application is maintained in one physical location, or replicated, where the shared application is copied to each collaborator site.

5.1.3.1 Centralized architecture / display broadcasting

The most common approach to implementing software distribution uses a centralized architecture, or display broadcasting, where only one copy of the application runs on any one of the participants' machines or on a central server. The inputs from the participants are forwarded to the application as if one single user provided them. Then the application handles these inputs, and the outputs of the application are intercepted and multicasted to all participants for display on their host.

Figure 34 shows two participants sharing one copy of an application. A central collaboration server receives all user input (1) and merges the events so that a single instance of the shared application receives a single stream of events (2). This application produces the display data (3) and the collaboration server then distributes the display updates to the participants' windowing systems (4).

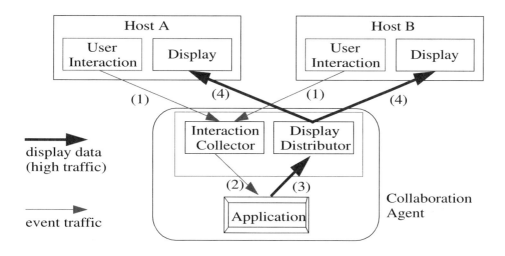

Figure 34: Centralized application sharing via display broadcasting

5.1.3.2 Replicated architecture / event broadcasting

In replicated collaboration-transparency architectures, also called event broadcasting, each participant has a copy of the shared application. The input from any participant is first captured and then multicasted to all copies of the application. So contrary to the centralized architecture, the participants don't receive the outputs of the shared application - that means a graphical representation of the shared application - but the input.

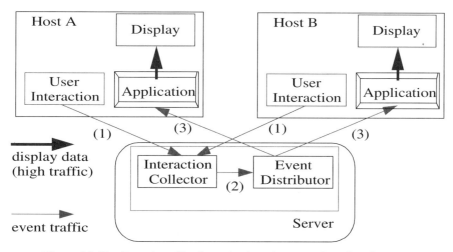

Figure 35: Replicated applications sharing via events broadcasting

Figure 35 illustrates the replicated architecture approach in which one component of a central collaboration agent centralizes the user events (1). The agent's job is then to multiplex the input events from any participating collaborator (2), and to broadcast them to the other collaborators (3). Finally each copy of the shared application processes the events (4).

5.1.3.3 Centralized versus replicated architecture

The main difference between the two architectures is the location where the shared application runs. This involves a distinction in the kind and in the quantity of data sent over the network. The replicated architecture has lower network traffic requirements than the centralized approach, because only the participants' input must be transmitted. Inputs are transmitted in both replicated and centralized architectures, but the centralized approach uses additional bandwidth to distribute the display information.

Having a copy of the shared application for each participant can lead to trouble for the replicated architecture. Indeed because multiple copies of the data exist, consistency is more difficult to guarantee than under centralized architecture, where only one instance of the application exists. The choice of the architecture depends also on the environment and the type of application that may be used in the collaboration session. For example, the display broadcasting fits naturally in a distributed windowing system like the X Window System that separates display from computation. However in sharing X applications [GWY94], both the centralized and replicated architectures can be used because it is easy to intercept both the input to and the output from the X applications.

On the other hand, in sharing Java applications only the user input events can be intercepted so that the replicated architecture is the only possible choice. Moreover the Java Virtual Machine provides a homogeneous application environment across hardware platforms. Another feature helps also Java supporting a replicated architecture: the Java Object Serialization, part of the Java Core API (Application Program Interface) in version 1.1, that is an object persistence mechanism and allows objects along with their states to be copied and transferred to remote participants.

5.2 Related Work

Many research teams and commercial companies are working on collaborative tools for application sharing. Traditionally, collaboration-transparency systems are able to share any application written to the standard API of a particular operating/windowing system, such as the X Window System or Microsoft Windows. On the other side Java application sharing is often based on a replicated architecture [EKFS99] and [ESGS00]. Such tools can run in different operating systems and the collaboration is either aware or transparent. In the following several collaborative systems will be discussed.

5.2.1 SharedX

Hewlett Packard's SharedX [GWY94] is a collaboration system that is based on the X Window System, introduced in 1987. The X Window system, known simply as X, is a networked window system allowing X applications running on one computer to display on another. To support this feature, X defines a graphics protocol that separates an application's display from its process. An application's process, called an X client (client is potentially a remote host), sends graphics requests to the display server, called an X server. The X server then returns the display information to the workstation.

This separation of display, process, and network transparency yield a natural approach to implementing collaboration transparency by intercepting and distributing an X client's display requests to multiple X servers. SharedX is based on this centralized approach by retransmitting the X protocol stream to multiple X display stations, thus simultaneously displaying application on multiple computer displays.

5.2.2 JVTOS

Joint Viewing and Tele-Operation Service (JVTOS) [DGO+94] provides an environment for telecooperation across high-speed networks. At its core lies the concept of application sharing. Users interact simultaneously with shared applications by jointly viewing them and by generating input to them. JVTOS enhances the sharing concept by two cooperation tools. A picturephone enables users to directly interact via audio and video channels. A telemarker tool allows them to point at objects viewed jointly.

JVTOS architecture defines three independent service modules: application sharing, picturephone, and telepointing. The first two of these are supported by a unified audio/video communication service. The JVTOS Session Management integrates these modules into the current JVTOS service.

JVTOS has two special features. First, it allows sharing of applications generating audio and video output. Second, it is implemented on three different platforms, namely Unix-based workstations, Macintosh, and MS-Windows computers. In this way, a platform independent service is realised allowing telecooperation for wide user groups.

5.2.3 NetMeeting

NetMeeting [Cor] is Microsoft's collaboration tool. It includes support for international conferencing standards and provides multi-user program sharing and data conferencing capabilities. It runs only on Windows operating systems. NetMeeting [Cor] supports among others the following applications:

- Video Conferencing and Internet Telephony.
- Chat and whiteboard: real time collaboration via text and graphic information.
- Program Sharing: flexibly sharing of multiple programs during a conference.
- Remote Desktop Sharing: operating a computer from a remote location.
- File Transfer: sending of files in the background during a collaboration.

NetMeeting functions as both a client and a platform. The NetMeeting client provides users the benefits of real-time audio, video, and multipoint data conferencing. The NetMeeting platform also provides software API support so that software developers can integrate these conferencing features into their own products and services.

NetMeeting's application collaboration is based on a centralized architecture. Users share the same view so that only one participant needs to have the program installed on its computer. The participant that shares one of its applications chooses to allow or to prevent others from working in the shared program. A major drawback of NetMeeting is its moderation capability. It allows only one person at a time can interact with a shared program.

The job of NetMeeting is to distribute graphics information via the ITU-T.128 protocol. This protocol specifies how participants in a ITU-T.120 conference can share local programs. Specifically, ITU-T.128 enables multiple conference participants to view and collaborate on shared programs by defining a graphics protocol that is conceptually similar to the X protocol. Thus, it facilitates the display broadcasting.

Other products conform to ITU-T.128, for example PictureTel's LiveShare Plus (PictureTel Corporation, 1997) and can therefore receive each other's display. ITU-T.128-compliant clients have been implemented on X, Windows, and Macintosh, but ITU-T.128 application-sharing servers currently exist only on Windows.

5.2.4 JCE

The Java Collaborative Environment (JCE) has been developed at the National Institute of Standards and Technology (NIST). JCE [AWFKK97] offers a groupware toolkit and an API for the development of application especially for collaboration. This tool is an aware collaboration one. But the required extra effort to make applications collaborative is not very high. Indeed JCE uses an extended version of the Java-AWT [AWFKK98] called Collaborative AWT (C-AWT). And the only modification to do is to replace the Java AWT package java.awt by the modified collawt package. That means that the JCE collaborative application imports that collawt and uses the corresponding C-AWT components.

5.2.5 Habanero

NCSA Habanero [CGJ+98] is an approach that supports the development of collaborative environments. Habanero is in its terms a framework that helps developers to create shared applications, either by developing a new one from scratch or by altering an existing single-user application which has to be modified to integrate the new collaborative functionality. Instead of using applets, which can be embedded in almost every browser, the Habanero system uses so-called "Happlets" which need a proprietary browser to be downloaded and installed on the client site.

5.2.6 JAMM

Java Applets Made Multiuser (JAMM) [BSSS97] is a system, which provides a transparent collaboration of single-user applications. But the set of applications that can be shared is constrained to those that are developed using Swing user interface components as part of Java Foundation Classes, which are part of the standard JDK since version 1.2. JAMM's set of applications is furthermore restricted to those, which implement the Java serializable interface. Indeed JAMM [BS98] uses an image-copy scheme provided by Java Object Serialization (JOS) to send the current state of a shared application to new comers. JOS is part of the core Java 1.1 class library and provides the means to copy an object's current state for storage or network transfer.

5.2.7 JETS

The Java-Enabled Telecollaboration System (JETS) [SOG98], [SG97], has been developed at the Multimedia Communications Research Laboratory (MCRLab) at the University of Ottawa, Canada, under funding from the national Telelearning Network of Centers of Excellence. JETS is a collaboration aware framework. It does not support transparent sharing of applications and applets, without modifying their source code.

JETS [SG97] is a framework that permits sharing of Java applets. Since JETS uses the core Java packages, users don't need to install any additional Java classes on their system. This allows any user to access JETS and share applets with a Java-enabled browser. From a developer's point of view, JETS can be regarded as a set of Application Programming Interfaces (API) that the developer can use to build shared resources. It provides the developer with built-in consistency, access control, and data passing.

5.2.8 DyCE

Dynamic Collaborative Environment (DyCE) developed at the Integrated Publication and Information Systems Institute (GMD-IPSI) [TS00] is a framework for the development of component-based groupware environments. Its architecture is based on dynamic object replication. The separation between the implementation of components and the shared domain objects manipulated by the components aids the combination of different components and the use of shared artifacts in evolving collaborative process. DyCE provides an API in order to implement collaborative applications. The main difference between DyCE and the proposed tool here is that DyCE is collaborative aware framework, which does not support sharing collaboration-unaware applications.

5.2.9 Java Remote Control Tool

There are many Java-based collaboration systems, none of which offer a management or moderation feature similar to ours. Kuhmünch [KFS98] at the University of Mannheim developed a Java Remote Control Tool, which allows the control and synchronization of distributed Java applications and applets. The drawback of this approach is that it is necessary to have access to the original source code of the application or applets in order to make it collaborative. That means every applet must initiate a Remote-Control-Client object, which is usually done in the constructor of the applet. Also the event handling within the applet must be modified in order to receive and/ or send events from / to remote applets. The Java Shared Data Toolkit (JSDT) from JavaSoft is also an API-based framework [TSDT00].

5.2.10 Lessons Learned

A problem with many collaborative applications [SEGS01a], [SEGS01b], [ESGS00], [SG97] is their platform dependence leading to the fact that users communicating in heterogeneous environments are restricted in their choice of a cooperative application. For example some users might choose UNIX-workstations, while others might prefer Windows 95/98/NT or Macintosh. But with the introduction of Java it became possible to overcome these problems. Consequently diverse approaches emerged which used Java for developing collaborative systems, producing a variety of toolkits and platforms [Inc95], [CGJ+98], [AWFKK97], and [BSSS97]. However, almost every system described in the literature requires the use of an API, or tries to replace some core Java-components with self-defined collaborative components. Moreover in conventional collaboration systems all participants see exactly the same view at the same time because the centralized application sends the same display information to all participants. This strict what you see is what I see (WYSI-WIS) may be not well suited to some applications and learning situations.

All the approaches [KFS98], [SOG98], [BSSS97], [CGJ+98], [AWFKK98] reviewed in the literature propose the use of an API, which has the cost of modifying the source-code of an application, re-implementing it or to design and implement a new application from scratch in order to make it collaborative. While this is double most of the time (see section 4.5.2), it is sometimes difficult or impossible to modify the source code of a resource. A lot of other systems (NetMeeting) are restricted to a specified Platform [Cor]. Moreover in conventional collaboration-transparency systems all participants see exactly the same view at the same time because the centralized application sends the same display information to all participants (SharedX). There's therefore a need for a system that can transparently share resources without the need to modify the code for the resource (req. #5). This system will be described in the following section.

5.3 JASMINE's System Architecture

The approach presented in this Chapter differs from other approaches in the way that neither a new API for developing collaborative systems is proposed nor replacement of core components at run time is tried. In fact a great variety of well-designed educational application already exist on the world wide web, which were developed to be run as stand-alone and it would not be acceptable or possible for many developers to re-implement or change these programs to make them work in a collaborative way. The practicality of the architecture presented here is proven by an implementation. A collaboration system, called Java Application Sharing in Multiuser INteractive Environment (JASMINE) was developed. JASMINE facilitates the creation of multimedia collaboration sessions and enables users to share applications, which are either pre-loaded or brought into the session live (req. #5). The system also provides basic utilities for session moderation and floor control. Furthermore, JASMINE enable diverse views of the same visualization in a moderated session (req. #6). This is useful if the moderator like a teacher wants his counterparts such as students to watch less than he can watch.

5.3.1 Aims and Features

Jasmine architecture is based on the Java Events Delegation Model [FE99]. This model provides a standard mechanism for a source component to generate an event and send it to a set of listeners. Furthermore, the event model also allows to send the event to an adapter, which then works as an event listener for the source and as a source for the listener. Because the handling of events is a crucial task in developing an application, this enhancement makes the development of applets much more flexible and the control of the events much more easy. The JASMINE architecture satisfies the following requirements for collaborative tools:

- *No source code modification should be allowed*:
  Indeed there are a lot of well designed learning animations (applets) world wide. It will be not accepted to modify the source code of these applications in order to use them collaboratively (req. #5).

- *As less as possible of the network's bandwidth should be consumed*:
  In a collaborative learning scenario, the learner and the students may use the network of their university but this scenario also includes interaction with students being at home. Moreover the customer support for an e-commerce business applies in part to customers at home. The collaborative session should therefore develop with satisfying performance with a limited bandwidth. Indeed, if the interaction is not responsive enough, the customer may become frustrated and walk away.

- *A collaboration session should not be limited to an operating system*:
  Considering the fact that the participants of a web collaborative session can utilize the operating system they want, it is absolutely necessary that the sharing tool doesn't restrict itself to one platform (req. #3).

- *Support for different views of the same visualization in a collaborative environment*:
  Using metadata discussed in Chapter 4 to give different views of the same problem to different persons. For example, a professor can see more options and have more control of a resource, whereas students can see fewer options and have less control opportunities (req. #6).

5.3.2 Main Idea

The principal idea of JASMINE is that user events occurring through the interaction with the GUI of an application or an applet can be caught, distributed, and reconstructed, hence allowing for Java applications to be shared transparently. This form of collaboration enables users to interact in real-time, working remotely as a team without caring about low-level issues, such as networking details [EKFS99], [ESGS00].

Figure 36 illustrates the overall concept of Jasmine, where the Jasmine collaboration framework wraps around the application that is to be shared. The framework listens to all events occurring in the graphical user interface of the application and transmits these events to all other participants in order to be reconstructed there. The framework captures both AWT-based and Swing-based events. After capturing the event, it is sent to the Jasmine collaboration agent (Jasmine-Server) where the event is sent to all other participants in the session.

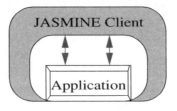

Figure 36: JASMINE's main concept

In the next sections we are going to discuss the architecture in more details, first the communication module (JASMINE server), and then the client side.

5.3.3 Server Architecture

The communications module's main purpose is to receive events from the collaboration manager and propagate them to all participants in the session. It abstracts the network and communication functionalities from the client side so that the client side need not worry about how the events are actually transmitted over the network. This module is separated from the rest of the system because it can be implemented in many different ways based on the communication environment. As mentioned earlier, reliability is a non-negotiable requirement for collaborative applications since loosing even one event can potentially disrupt the collaboration session. This means that the communication module must be implemented by either reliable multicast (RM) or TCP.

Each of these approaches has certain advantages and disadvantages. The obvious disadvantage of the one-to-one TCP linking approach is scalability: the more users there are, the more network connections are required. What's worse is that the number of connections increases non-linearly with increasing number of users. However, using a client-server approach can substantially decrease the number of network connections. Each client establishes a TCP connection only to the server as opposed to each and every other client. The server then becomes responsible for sending messages between users. The main disadvantage of a server-based approach is the additional delay caused by the server's processing of the incoming events, which sometimes makes the server the bottleneck of the system.

There are many advantages in using RM for the implementation of the communication module. RM technology uses substantially less bandwidth and produces lower delays than a TCP-client-server based approach. But the disadvantages of the RM approach are practical ones, not theoretical ones. All RM technologies available are based on UDP multicast. Multicast support in today's Internet is far from acceptable and in fact today's Internet leaves a lot to be desired when it comes to multicasting. The Mbone tries to compensate this lack of adequate support, but even then a great portion of a multicast session's traffic are "tunneled" through the non-multicast portions of the Internet. In addition, joining and maintaining Mbone connectivity is not a trivial task; one cannot expect ordinary users to easily connect to the Mbone. Furthermore, RM technology is still maturing and standards are still being made. As a result there are many incompatible RM implementations today but mostly for research/experimentation purposes [Obr98].

With JASMINE, our main goal is to create a system that can be accessed by the most number of people and in fact that's why we chose the Java technology. From practical stand-point, it makes little sense to implement the communication module in such a way that most ordinary Internet users won't be able to use it, or will have to go through a great deal of connection set-up just to use our system. We therefore decided to implement the communication module with a TCP-client-server design. As we will see later in the performance evaluation section, the performance of this design is quite adequate for small to medium-sized group collaboration sessions.

JASMINE uses a multithreaded server, where the main server launches a sub-server for each user joining the session. The sub-server is responsible for processing only the update messages or requests coming in from its own client. Once the sub-server receives the update message, it will send it to all other clients in the session (figure 6). This will create a fast system response, at the expense of more resources utilized due to sub-server threads. However, usually only one client at a time can control and interact with an application (due to floor control as we will see), and most threads will simply be waiting and won't consume too much resources.

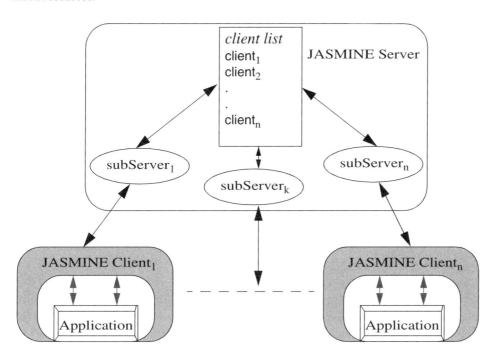

Figure 37: JASMINE's client-server architecture

The server's main job is to propagate the incoming events from a user to all other users. But it also provides other services, which are necessary for maintaining a collaboration session.

It provides services for session moderation and management, floor control, and data exchange. Data exchange is of particular importance for multimedia sessions as we will see next.

5.3.4 Client Architecture

The JASMINE client [EKFS99] and [SEGS01a] can be seen as a component adapter. Every event occurring at the graphical user interface of the application is sent to this adapter, which then sends the events to the collaboration server (JASMINE-Server). The client is a Java application, which consists of the following components:

- Collaboration Manager
- Listener Adapter
- Component Adapter
- Event Adapter

These components are discussed next.

5.3.4.1 Collaboration Manager

The Collaboration Manager is the main component on the client side. It is responsible for the communication between the Jasmine Client and the Jasmine Server. Therefore it provides the user with a graphical interface offering options such as joining the session, starting and sharing applications, and chatting with other participants. After a successful registration to a session, the Collaboration Manager creates a connection to the Jasmine Server.

Then the Collaboration Manager is responsible for dispatching external events coming from the communication module and forwarding them to the component adapter, as well as receiving internal events from the component adapter and sending them to the communication module. It receives two sorts of events: system events and user events. The system events are handled directly by the Collaboration Manager. They are either ChatEvents, events that contains chat messages, or UserEvents, events that gives information about the participants.

5.3.4.2 Listener Adapter

The Listener Adapter implements several AWT listeners, which listen to MouseEvent and KeyEvent for all AWT-components except of java.awt.Scrollbar, java.awt.Choice, and java.awt.List. For these components the Listener Adapter listens to AdjustmentEvent, ItemEvent, and ActionEvent. When an event occurs on the GUI of the application, the Listener Adapter catches it and converts it to an external event. Such an external event is called a RemoteAWTEvent. It contains a local event and information about the sender and the corresponding application and GUI component.

After catching an event, the Listener Adapter controls it to filter the Remote events. Then it forwards the event to the Collaboration Manager if it has been locally fired. The Collaboration Manager in turn sends this event to the Communication Module, which propagates the event to all other participants via the server.

5.3.4.3 Components Adapter

The Component Adapter maintains a list of references to the GUI-components of all applications and applets. This list is created with the help of the java.awt.Container class, which allows us to get references of all application components. With the help of the main window of an application, a list of the GUI components in the application can directly be created. Therefore, the main window of an application loaded by the Collaboration Manager is registered by the Component Adapter. However, Java applets do not use stand-alone windows. They are an extension of the class java.applet.Applet and thus of java.awt.Panel. Hence, applets can be easily placed into a window, which can then be registered as the main window for the applet. All these registrations of applets and applications are done at the Component Adapter during the session or at the beginning of the session thank a property file.

After the registration is completed, a list of all Swing and/or AWT-components within the loaded application/applet is created. This task is done in the same order on each client, so that a component has the same reference identification at all clients. These references are used to point to specific components, which are the source of the events generated internally and the recipient of the events generated externally. With the help of the references, the recipient of an incoming event is located and the event is reconstructed on each client, as if it occurred locally.

An example syntax of the registration by the Component Adapter is shown in Figure 5.

```
....
Class cl = Class.forName(className);
// If it is an applet, instantiate and locate
// it in a Frame
myApplet = (Applet)cl.newInstance();
myApplet.init();
myWindow = new Frame("Titel");
myWindow.add("Center", myApplet);
// Otherwise (if it is an instance of Window) just
// instantiate it
myWindow = (Window)cl.newInstance();
// Register this Frame as main Frame
// by Components Adapter
ComponentsAdapter.addContainer(myWindow);
...
```

Listing 5: Excerpt of the instantiating method

5.3.4.4 Event Adapter

The Event Adapter works opposite to the Listener Adapter. It converts incoming external events to events that can then be processed locally. The events sent from the server contain only a reference on the component, which is the source of the event. The Component Adapter finds out the corresponding component and container, if necessary, and gives these to the Event Adapter as parameter. The Event Adapter next reconstructs an event and forwards it to the application.

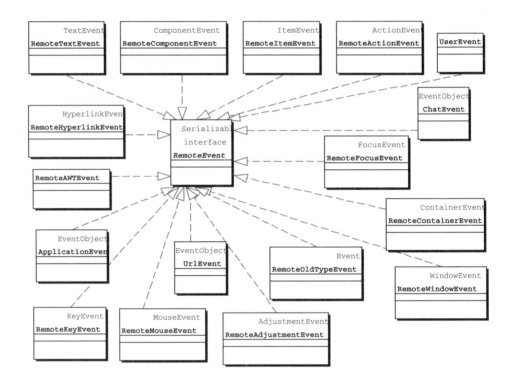

Figure 38: UML Class Diagram of JASMINE Events

The Event Adapter does not reconstruct the AWT Events directly, but constructs session specific events. These events are the extensions of the corresponding AWT Events and implement the RemoteEvent Interface, so that the locally created AWT Events can be distinguished from those created by the other clients. This event communication is based on an extensible hierarchy of event classes. The root of this hierarchy as can be seen in Figure 38 is the serializable class RemoteEvent. These RemoteEvents shown in the UML class diagram are:

- RemoteActionEvent (component-defined action occurs)
- RemoteAdjustmentEvent (adjustment event is emitted)
- RemoteComponentEvent (component becomes visible)
- RemoteContainerEvent (container's contents changed because a component was added or removed)
- RemoteFocusEvent (component gets the keyboard focus)

116 ▪ Chapter 5 Collaborative Use of Instructional Visualizations

- RemoteHyperlinkEvent (hyperlink is selected)
- RemoteItemEvent (item is selected or deselected)
- RemoteKeyEvent (key is pressed, released, or typed)
- RemoteMouseEvent (user presses a mouse button)
- RemoteOldTypeEvent (JDK 1.0 Event Model)
- RemoteTextEvent (text of an object such as a TextComponent changed)
  RemoteWindowEvent (user closes a frame)

5.3.5 Data Flow

Let us summarize the client side's architecture through the following data flow diagram. Figure 39 shows the overall event circulation of the system.

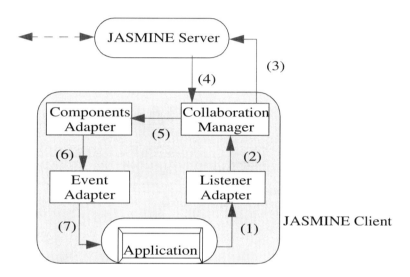

Figure 39: Events circulation

There are two main data paths in the system: the first path is labeled with numbers 1,2, and 3. This path is used to send the internal AWT events to the communication module, and it works as follows: any Event occurred in a Java-application is caught by the Listener Adapter. The Listener Adapter first tests whether the event is an external or an internal event. It then sends only the internal events, which were not received from other clients, to the Collaboration Manager, which in turn sends the events to the communication module.

Via the second data path shown in Figure 39 with numbers 4, 5, 6, and 7, the external AWT events received from the communication module are captured by the Collaboration Manager and the Component Adapter in order to reconstruct the events locally. After receiving the remote event, the Component Adapter extracts the information about its target component and sends this information together with the event to the Event Adapter. The Event Adapter converts the event to normal AWT event and sends it to the application, which then reacts to the event in the same manner as it would to a local user's interaction with the application's GUI.

5.4 JASMINE's Features

JASMINE facilitates user conversations by having a shared chat space which can be used by participants to exchange textual massages. The chat space is useful, e.g., in cases where students have some questions. Using a text input filed, one can type in the URL of any resource on the Web. That resource is then brought into the session dynamically and is shared among all participants in real time. In addition, a number of resources can be predefined before the session starts and can be started during the session from the "Tools" menu. Since any Java applet or application can be brought into the session, JASIMNE has a potential unlimited extendibility property, since each resource enhances JASMINE dynamically. JASMINE has a moderation capabilities allowing for dynamic and real-time moderation of a shared session.

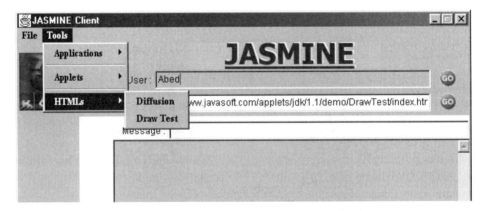

Figure 40: Graphical user interface of JASMINE client

As mentioned before the shared applets and applications are collaboration-unaware applications developed using the standard Java technology. These applications can be loaded dynamically, after a client joins a session, or can be downloaded on the fly during the session by typing in the URL of the desired applet. In the first case a specific number of preloaded applications/applets that a user can invoke must be stored in a configuration file before the start of the session (seeSection 5.4.1). In the second case, participants can just type the URL of the applet they want to bring into the environment to share. JASMINE then fetches the applet and inserts it into each client's session. There is no limit as to the number of simultaneous applets/applications running in the session.

5.4.1 Configuration File

Information about locally available applications and applets, which can be used in a collaborative way, are read from a configuration file. The configuration file, which is organized as a properties file, contains the names of the applications/applets, which will be presented in the menu and the full names of their main class or URL. The entries have the following syntax:

        application.[n].name = [name]
        application.[n].class = [class]

where:

        n: number of the application in the list.
        name: a suitable name for the application to be shown in the menu.
        class: full name of the main class.

An example configuration file is illustrated in Listing 6:

```
#Application entries
application.1.name=myTestApplication
application.1.class=kom.develop.apps.MyApplication
# Applet entries
applet.1.name=myTestApplet
applet.1.class=kom.develop.applets.MyApplet
# URL entries
url.1.name= myTestUrl
url.1.address=http://desiered.server/my.html
...
```

Listing 6: Excerpt from a configuration file

Before starting the session, applets and applications that are thought to be useful can be placed in this configuration file. Additional applets and applications can be brought into the session live as needed through the "URL field", described above.

5.4.2 Floor Control

A collaborative system must address many issues such as synchronization, latecomers, management or moderation, floor control, and awareness [SOG98]. Among these, floor control is perhaps the most primary issue without which a collaborative session won't function properly. In short, floor control ensures that only one person at a time controls the shared application. Without floor control, there will be collisions of events, which leads to unwanted results in the shared application.

In JASMINE, floor control is achieved by means of locking. Each application has a corresponding *semaphore* on the server. When a user wants to interact with the shared application, the system first locks the application by locking a semaphore. At this point, any other users trying to interact with the application will be denied access. When the first user is finished, the system releases the semaphore and others can take control of the application.

For a specific shared application, most developers prefer an "intuitive" implementation of the floor control capability; i.e., as soon as the user tries to interact with the application, the client automatically asks for floor control and allows or disallows its user to interact. After the user is finished, the client releases the lock automatically. Listing 7 shows sample Java code that demonstrates how the floor control is used in an intuitive way. This approach is in contrast to the "direct" approach, where a client must specifically ask for control, for example by pressing a "control-request" button.

```
public void keyPressed(KeyEvent ke){
    // User is pressing a key, ask for control
    if (getControl() == true ) {
        // do whatever you want to do by pressing the key
        releaseControl();
    }
    else
        showErrorMessage(this.KEYPRESSED_ERROR_MESSAGE_EN);
...
```

Listing 7: Excerpt from the floor control class

Just how intuitive the approach in Listing 7 really is depends on the system response. If there is a small delay between the time the user tries to interact and the time when something actually happens on the screen, the application is intuitive. If however that delay is large, the application becomes "unnatural". So the Floor Control Delay (FCD) is an interesting parameter that we must also evaluate.

5.4.3 Moderation

Although floor control addresses the issue of event collisions, it works on a first-come-first-serve basis. This in turn leads to the possibility of a participant to abuse or disrupt the session by feeding unwanted events into the session. There is therefore a need to have a moderator in order for a session to be more productive, for example, a teacher moderating a distance learning session. The moderator is usually the person who calls for a collaborative session and starts the server. In JASMINE we have two types of sessions: moderated, and non-moderated. The server can be started by specifying a login name and password for the moderator. Once the session starts, the moderator can login at any time and take control of the session. When the session is moderated, no one can send any events to the server. A participant wishing to do so must ask for permission from the moderator as shown in Figure 41a. The moderator will subsequently receive a message indicating the participant's request to interact (Figure 41b) which the moderator can allow or refuse. Upon moderator's acceptance of the user's request, the user will receive a green light, which indicates that he or she can now send events to the session (Figure 41c). The moderator can also dynamically "cut off" a user's permission to interact if needed (Figure 41d). In JASMINE, we allow only one user at a time to have permission to send events, although this number can be increased based on the application.

JASMINE can be further enhanced using dynamic metadata discussed in Chapter 4 to simultaneously give different views of the same problem to different persons. For example, a professor can see more options and have control of a resource, whereas students can see fewer options and have less control opportunities. This issue will be discussed next.

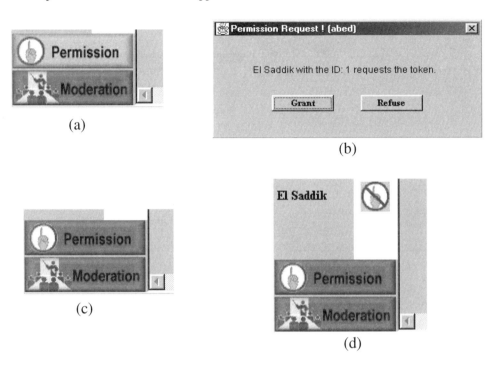

(a)

(b)

(c)

(d)

Figure 41: Moderation capabilities in JASMINE

5.5 Sharing Different Views of the Same Visualization

The issue of having several alternative views in distributed system will be investigated in this section. When a student wishes to interact with the instructor with some specific questions, the instructor may find it appropriate to co-share material from the lecture with the student. But allowing the student to see less he by himself can. This is appropriate when the material has different complexity levels (DifficultiLevel as explained Chapter 4). This feature is also very useful in engineering where the worker on site may have some information displayed on his mobile device, while the engineer in the main office may have a detailed explanation on the screen.

Reusable instructional visualizations can be developed according to the component based framework enhanced with metadata described in the previous Chapter. Dynamic metadata allows to reuse the same visualization in different context according to the user needs and wishes. One possible solution is to allow multiple views of the same dynamic

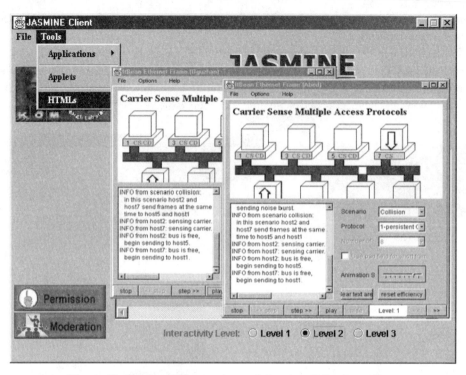

Figure 42: Sharing different views of the same Ethernet applet

learning object. The interactivity level and the view is different between the participants but the underlaying model is the same (MVC-Architecture discussed in Chapter 3). For instance using the proposed metadata field explanation allows the teacher to have, e.g., textual explanation, while the student just watch the animation. or using the field hints give the student the possibility to think about what is going to happen in the visualization. In order to proof this idea we further enhanced JASMINE client to understand and deal with queries contained the metadata fields proposed in Chapter 5. Figure 42 shows how a visualization (Ethernet applet discussed earlier in this thesis) is shared in a moderated session. In the left picture the interactivity level of the end user is given to 1 those the possible scenarios to be shown are restricted to two ("normal operation" and collision) while the moderator (the right picture) started the visualization in the 3rd interactivity level and those he is able to choose more scenarios and have more interaction possibilities with the system. For instance the teacher may choose to start the visualization after clicking on the choicebox "use pad field for short frame". The visualization at all other participant will than change its behaviour according to this choice. The teacher may then ask through JASMINE's whiteboard some questions, and those tries to challenge his students interactively while doing it over distance.

Having different views, while running the same visualization can be achieved by passing different parameter to the users in a JASMINE session. To achieve such a functionality. The visualizations should be implemented according to the iTBeanKit Framework described in the previous Chapter.

5.5.1 Shared Browsing

It is know obvious that JASMINE not only support the sharing of applications without modifying their source code, but also support having different views of one problem. Indeed some times it is necessary to share a web page with different view. Collaborative web browsing allows a group of users to surf the web together. The users could be geographically distributed and possibly working on different platforms. In this environment when a user in the group loads a new document from a site, the same documents gets loaded on all the other users' web browsers.

Once again a possible approach is to use technologies based on the X Window System protocol like SharedX [GWY94] or technologies based on NetMeeting [Cor] under Windows. However, this approach is not amenable to a group of users working on multiple platforms like Unix, MacOS, and Windows.

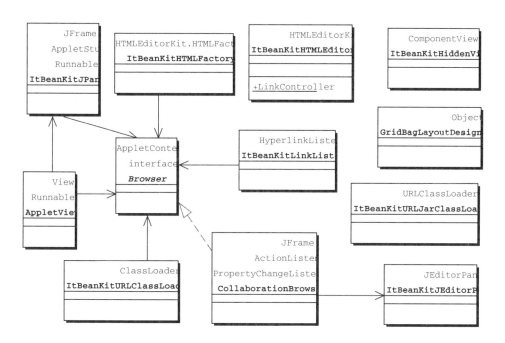

Figure 43: UML Class Diagram of JASMINE Browser

The developed browser support the metadata fields proposed in this work and thus able to browse different pages according to the level of difficulty the moderator wants the session to be moderated with. For instance it is possible to browse a lecture about a specific topic, and students from different background or terms may get different informations, if the lecture was described with the appropriate LOM set of metadata. As has been explained above, when navigation (changing the page) occurs on any browser, all other browser taking part in the session automatically follow. A navigation change can happen, by clicking on the navigation buttons (Forward, Backward, Stop, and Reload), by typing a desired URL in the appropriate text field or by clicking a link in the presented HTML page.

5.6 Performance Evaluation

JASMINE can be considered a real-time tool in the sense that its updating response time, in a network environment capable of supporting real-time applications, is within the acceptable parameters of human quality of service for desktop collaboration, as we shall see. But as with any TCP based multiuser system, there is an upper-bound to the number of simultaneous users before those parameters are violated. This "maximum users" limit depends on the resources utilized by the system, such as processing power, graphics power, memory, network bandwidth, and network delay, as well as the design of the communication part of the system.

Depending on the quality desired, the application level end-to-end delay between two users should be less than 1000 milliseconds, with 200 milliseconds recommended for tightly-synchronized tasks [Inc95]. However, these numbers are valid only if the shared application is used in conjunction with some type of media that provide a sense of presence such as video and audio. The reason is that if audio or video or both are present, users have a sense of "awareness" of each other, which in turn requires the shared application to respond within a time that maintains that awareness. For example, imagine three engineers who are collaboratively designing a bridge in a live session. One of them highlights a section of the bridge and says: "I think this part should be redesigned". If they are using real-time audio conferencing (end-to-end audio delay of 100 msec), then the delay of the shared application must comply with the above numbers in order for the other two engineers to receive the audio message and the event update in such a way as to maintain the real-time quality of the session. This is usually the case in controlled IP environments such as local networks networks.

In the case of typical Internet connections, where audio and video delays are not controllable, or in the absence of audio or video, restrict delay parameters make little sense because the users have no time-wise perception of one another. In such instances, when a user receives an update message, the user has no way of knowing when an actual action occurred. So, even a delay of 5 seconds or more might be acceptable depending on the nature of the application under such circumstances.

Our performance evaluations are done for a controllable environment, where real-time characteristics are required and can be supported.

5.6.1 Parameters of Interest

The most common parameter that measures the quality of a collaborative application is the Client-to-Client Delay (CCD). CCD tries to measure the average time it takes for an update message to reach other users. It includes all layers between the two clients, including application, transport, networking, data link, and physical layer delays. However, at the application level, it only measures the time it takes for a sender to send or a receiver to receive the update at the application layer. It does not include the delay caused by what the application does with the update because that is application-dependent. For example, when a line is drawn in a shared whiteboard, CCD measures the average delay from the time the sender application assembles and sends the update message until the time the receiver receives the message and extracts the data from it, just before it makes a graphics call to actually draw the line. Hence, for an overall delay, one must also add the average on-the-screen drawing time, referred to as Rendering Delay, which really depends on the capabilities of the graphics, memory, and processing power of various client machines and therefore not constant for all clients. As another example, if one user opens an image in a whiteboard, what we measure is how long it takes for the "open-image" message to reach all clients. We don't measure how long it takes for the receivers to actually download the image from a given URL and show it on their screen, because we can't control those delays and they are not related to the collaboration system shown in Figure 33.

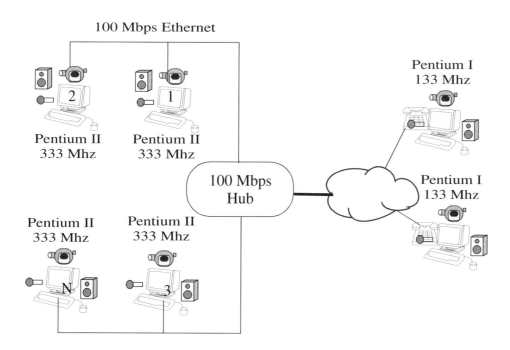

Figure 44: Network configuration for tests

As mentioned earlier, the server processing time per packet increases with increasing number of simultaneous users. This is due to one-to-one TCP connection-oriented nature of the system; the server needs to send the update info to each client one by one. This Server Processing Delay (SPD) adds to the overall end-to-end delay of the system and must be taken into account when calculating maximum number of users supported by the system.

Another interesting parameter is the Floor Control Delay (FCD). This is the average time for a user to take control or be denied taking control of an application and measures how intuitive a system is. A system with a smaller FCD is more "natural" and behaves more naturally than a system with a larger FCD.

5.6.2 Testing and Results

We tested CCD, SPD, and FCD of JASMINE over both local area network (LAN) and telephone modem access. During the testing, all machines were running their usual background processes related to the network and the operating system. The testing configuration is shown in Figure 44. All machines were running JDK 1.2 on Windows NT 4.0 Workstation. In addition, two 133 Mhz Pentium machine running Windows 95 were used to dial-in into the LAN with 28.8 kbps modems over phone lines. The result of the tests are shown next.

5.6.2.1 CCD Test

For the CCD test, we had a "sender" applet send an event to a "receiver" applet. Upon receiving the event, the receiver applet extracts all necessary data from the packet, reassembles the event, and sends the event back to the sender. The sender does the same thing and resends the event, and so on. This is repeated for a given duration, which was 10 minutes in our tests. The result of this test was an average CCD of 150 msec on the LAN, and 370 msec between the clients behind 28.8 kbps modem. It is worth mentioning that the transmission delay of the very first event took 750 msec and 2.5 sec on the LAN and modem, respectively. We believe this to be attributed to the Just-in-Time compiler (JIT) utility of JDK 1.2 which compiles the interpreted bytecode of a given method into native code, the first time that method is called, causing a one-time-only larger than usual delay.

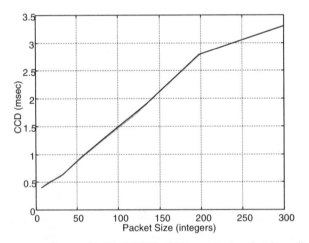

Figure 45: JASMINE CCD results (packet-based)

The system must also be able to send data between clients in addition to the event updates. It is interesting to know the delay of sending such data. We therefore repeated the CCD test for data exchange, this time for data of different packet sizes. The result is shown is Figure 45.

The packet size is measured in number of integers sent per packet. Even though it is very unlikely that a synchronization or control message of size 500 integers is sent in one packet, we did extend our test to that limit to see the effect of very large update messages. Figure 46 shows the same test performed over 28.8 Kbps modem access instead of 100 Mbps Ethernet.

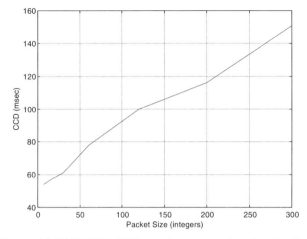

Figure 46: JASMINE CCD results over modem line (packet-based)

5.6.2.2 SPD Test

For the SPD test, we had the sender applet flood the server with event updates. Then we had the receivers (up to 45) calculate the average delay between receiving adjacent packets from the server. As expected, this delay increases with increasing number of users as seen in Figure 47.

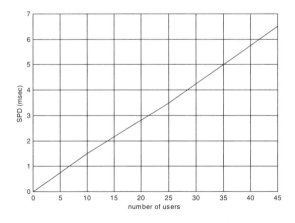

Figure 47: JASMINE Server Processing Delay

Figure 48 shows the same test performed for data updates. Note that due to floor control and moderation, no more that one client at a time can send events to the server, a scenario, which is typical of collaborative applications.

We can see that the delay increases linearly. This is due to the fact that the server spends equal amount of processing time per packet per client; therefore it increases linearly with increasing number of clients.

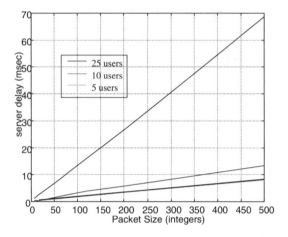

Figure 48: JASMINE Server Processing Delay (data)

5.6.2.3 FCD Test

For the Floor Control Delay, we had a client constantly ask for control, and release it upon receipt, for a given amount of time. The average FCD turned out to be less than 5 msec, which affirms the intuitiveness of the floor-control mechanism of the system.

5.6.3 Subjective evaluation

We also tested some applets, including a typical whiteboard application, as seen in Figure 49, with up to 5 users sitting next to each other and able to see one another's screens. The applications responded in a natural manner in terms of the feel and interaction/perception of the diverse shared applications. The visual updating delay between the screens of the workstations was very small yet detectable by the naked eye. Figure 49 illustrates a sample screenshot of a typical JASMINE session, where arbitrary applets and resources from the Internet have been brought into the session dynamically.

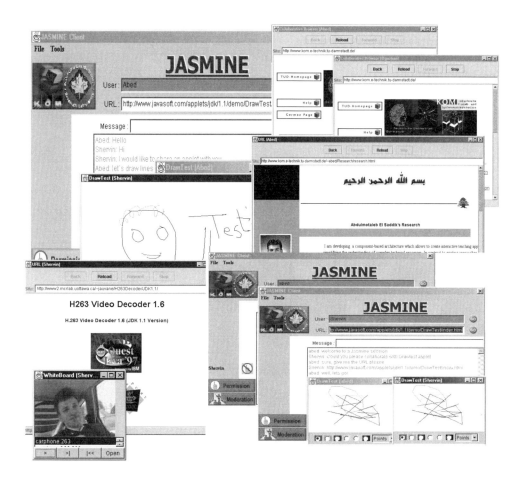

Figure 49: Screenshot of a JASMINE session

5.6.4 Analysis

As mentioned before, the recommended overall end-to-end delay is less than 1000 msec, with less than 200 msec required for closely-coupled collaboration. This delay includes the CCD, the SPD, and the on-screen rendering/display delay corresponding to the application's GUI. As argued previously, the rendering delay (RD) is not constant and it depends on the hardware/OS/platform used.

From the CCD and SPD tests, we can approximate the overall delay as:

delay = CCD + SPD + RD;

from Figure 47: SPD ≈ 0.142* N, where N is the number of users;

hence:

delay ≈ CCD + 0.142* N + RD

which roughly represents the delay experienced from the time an event is generated due to a client's interaction until that interaction is shown on the screen of all other clients. Figure 50 shows achievable number of users based on the expected overall delay, for different rendering delays (RD).

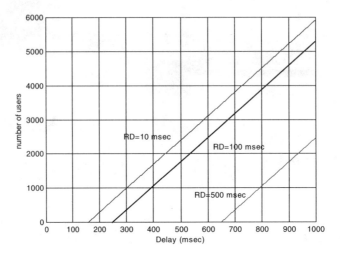

Figure 50: Number of users supported by the system

Figure 51 shows the same thing with focus on tightly-synchronized tasks (delay<200 msec).

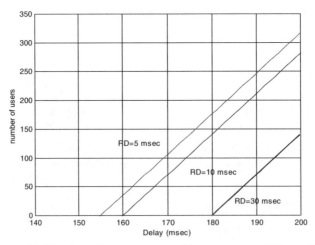

Figure 51: Number of users supported by the system (delay < 200 msec)

Finally, Figure 52 illustrates number of users supportable with 28.8 Kbps modem access.

130 ▪ Chapter 5 Collaborative Use of Instructional Visualizations

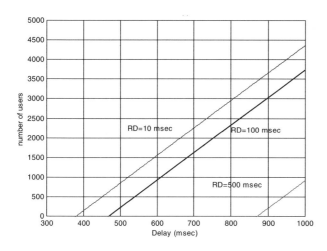

Figure 52: Number of users supported by the system (modem access)

By looking at the above graphs, we can conclude that the system can support "many" users. Even though the plots suggest that theoretically thousands of users can be supported, the fact is that the actual number of users supportable is less. The reason is that the linear behavior of the system diminishes as the number of users increase: the performance of the machine running the server decreases substantially as we approach the limit of maximum allowable socket connections on the machine, also the underlying physical network becomes slower with increasing number of users. So the hardware/OS of the server machine and the network either cannot support so many simultaneous users, or their performance decreases significantly. Nevertheless, this shows that the underlying communication module of JASMINE can support small-size and medium-sized collaboration sessions of hundreds of users, resource permitting.

5.7 Summary

We presented the architecture and implementation of our transparent collaboration framework for reusing stand-alone application in a shared environment (req. #5). We developed this architecture in order for users to be able to collaborate via collaborative-unaware applications and applets without modifying the source code. Our architecture enables us to use almost all single-user applets and applications in a collaborative way. We have successfully tested our system on a number of applications. We also observed that using the TCP-client-server approach of our communication module can support relatively large number of users.

Having the same application appearing in different places has several advantages. It reduces cost and development time (req. #1) and improves usability (req. #4). To share diverse views of the same application in a moderated session (req. #6), dynamic metadata presented in the previous Chapter were used. Thus the same visualizations, developed according to the component-based process enhanced with dynamic metadata, can be used and reused in the transparent shared environment. This novel idea was also presented in this Chapter, accompanied with implemntation and a usage scenario.

There are two outstanding issues remaining. These issues are not directly related to JAS-MINE but are research areas of the transparent collaboration paradigm. The first issue is that of latecomer-support. When a user starts a session later than other participants, there is a need to bring this user up-to-date as opposed to start from scratch. This can be achieved either by sending the entire object state of the shared application to the newcomer using object serialization, or by sending all the events occurred up to now to the new user so that it follows the same sequence of events that other participants have gone through.

Another issue concerns multimedia inter-client synchronization and control. As discussed in the literature, a pure transparent collaboration system is not sufficient for multimedia applications [SEGS01a]. This fact is due to specific services that are required by multimedia applications such as synchronization, quality of service, etc. For example, think of a collaboration session where a video applet is being played. When one user presses the pause button, simply capturing the "pause event" and sending it to all other clients is not sufficient because when other clients receive the pause event and apply it to their video player, at each client the video player will pause on a different frame and clients will not be synchronized. Hence there is a need to send control messages between clients, such as "pause on frame number 57" to maintain consistency among all users. The JASMINE server provides a high-level API that can be used for this type of advanced requirements. However, an application must specifically use the API to take advantage of these functionalities, hence the transparent feature of the system is somewhat diminished.

You either get it, or you don't
— Life Law #1

Chapter 6 Conclusions and Outlook

The production of interactive multimedia content is in most cases an expensive task in terms of time and cost. The goal of this work was hence, to optimize this production, by exploiting the reusability of interactive multimedia elements, as well as using and reusing available interactive visualizations in collaborative environments.

This work shows by example, that reusability can be achieved by a combination of reusable multimedia components, together with appropriate use of metadata to control those components as well as their combination.

A component-based framework (iTBeanKit) has been developed as a part of the Multibook project, to reuse and facilitate the combination of programming code. It guarantees the unified user interface and interaction facilities of instructional visualizations. This framework offers the developer basic classes and components which can be used to produce interactive multimedia learning modules. The visual representation of the developed multimedia learning modules looked alike for all interactive elements (applets). To describe instructional visualizations properly and to integrate them into an appropriate learning context according to the learner's needs, a new set of metadata is introduced, which is an extension of LOM. Having explained the necessary category of dynamic metadata, the implementation of the tools which can be used for tagging, storing, and customizing instructional visualizations is described. As a prototype, visualization artifacts dealing with the network protocol "CSMA/CD (Ethernet)" was implemented. Evaluation studies dealing with the tailorability of instructional visualizations as well as their usability have been conducted. As a result we observed that the customizability of the applet to use and reuse it in different learning context with dynamic metadata was accepted by the users. The users learned about multimedia communications technology, not about using a program. Thus, the usability does not suffer from the reusability.

Although collaboration tools have existed for a long time, Internet-based multimedia collaboration has recently received a lot of attention mainly due to easy accessibility of the Internet by ordinary users. However most of these systems require the shared application to be re-written according to the collaboration system's Application Programming Interface

(API) - a task which is sometimes difficult or even impossible. In this work, a practical approach for transparent collaboration is also presented (sharing collaboration un-aware applications). This mechanism uses event broadcasting to enable the collaboration. It is more efficient than the existing ones in terms of reusing stand-alone applications downloaded on each participant of the collaboration, instead of having one application runing on a central host. It wraps existing applications with a layer to achieve collaboration transparency without source code modification. Furthermore, and based on the dynamic metadata, sharing of different views of the same application in a moderated collaborative session is introduced, making it a novel approach. Our implementation of theses mechanisms, JASMINE has been successfully deployed and tested in shared sessions. Based on our experience, an interesting part of the system is the moderation from the user perspective. This enables a useful and practical session to be carried out without interruptions. Furthermore it allows the sharing of different views of the same object. This feature, for instance, simplifies educator's work, while it allows to test the knowledge of his students using the same multimedia content. The ability to dynamically bring almost any resource into a JASMINE session is another key feature enjoyed and emphasized by all users.

Our experience suggests that the visualizations offered by the developed system may well provide an environment in which an educator without conventional programming skills can build a useful interactive visual algorithm relevant to a particular task. The systems will therefore continue to be extended, particularly by increasing the available choice of visualization units. Currently iTBeanKit is being used to develop other examples of teaching animations for the multimedia and communications courses of the Department of Electrical Engineering and Information Technology at Darmstadt University of Technology (Germany), and Universidad de La Plata (Argentina), for example animations to explain multimedia scheduling algorithms.

Another activity which should be taken into consideration for further development, is that of sharing applications, having different views, among heterogeneous end devices (Desktop PC, PDA, UMTS-devices, etc.). This feature could be very useful in engineering where a worker on site may have some information displayed on his mobile device, while the chef engineer in the main office may have a detailed explanation on the screen.

This work is intended to become a starting point towards the development of metadata which are suitable to describe any type of instructional content, extending the traditional understanding of static metadata. We are well aware of the fact that such a standardization is a complex process and would like to initiate a discussion in that area.

Abbreviations

Apache	A "patchy" server, a public domain Web server from the Apache Group
ANSI	American National Standards Institute
Applet	A small application, such as a utility program or limited-function spreadsheet or word processor. (Java applet)
API	Application Programming Interface
ARIADNE	Alliance of Remote Instructional Authoring and Distribution Networks for Europe
ASAS	Actor Script Animation Language
ASCII	American Standard Code for Information Interchange
ASP	Active Server Page
BALSA	Brown Algorithmic Simulator and Animator
BML	Bean Markup Language
CAD	Computer Aided Design
CASE	Computer Aided Software Engineering
CBD	Component-based software development
CBT	Computer Based Training
CCD	Client to Client Delay
CD-ROM	Compact Disc-Read Only Memory
CGI	Common Gateway Interface
COM	Component Object Model
CSCL	Computer Supported Collaborative Learning
CSCW	Computer Supported Collaborative Work
CSMA/CD	Carrier Sense Multiple Access with Collision Detection
DBMS	Data Base Management System
DC	Dublin Core
DCT	Discrete Cosine Transformation

DFT	Discrete Fourier Transformation
DIS	Distributed Interactive Simulation
DIS	Draft International Standard (at ISO)
DTD	Document Type Definition
EJB	Enterprise JavaBeans
FCD	Floor Control Delay
FDCT	Fast Discrete Cosine Transformation
FFT	Fast Fourier Transformation
FTP	File Transfer Protocol
GIF	Graphical Interchange Format
HTML	HyperText Markup Language
HTTP	HyperText Transfer Protocol
IDCT	Inverse Discrete Cosine Transformation
IDE	Integrated Development Environments
IEEE	Institute of Electrical and Electronics Engineers
IMS	Instructional Management System
I/O	Input/Output
iTBeanKit	interactive Teaching Bean Kit
IP	Internet Protocol
J2EE	Java 2 platform Enterprise Edition
JASMINE	Java Application Sharing in Multiuser INteractive Environment
JPEG	Joint Pictures Expert Group
JVM	Java Virtual Machine
LAN	Local Area Network
LOM	Learning Object Metadata
LTSC	Learning Technology Standards Committee
Meta data	Data that describes other data
MIME type	Multipurpose Internet Mail Extensions
MPEG	Motion Pictures Expert Group
MVC	Model View Controller
OLE	Object Linking and Embeding
OMG	Object Management Group
OOA	Object Oriented Analyses
OOD	Object Oriented Design
OOP	Object Oriented Programming
ORB	Object Request Broker
OS	Operating System
Perl	Practical Extraction Report Language

RGB	Red-Green-Blue
RMI	Java Remote Method Invocation
RMP	Reliable Multicast Protocol
RPC	Remote Procedure Call
RSVP	Resource Reservation Protocol
SPD	Server Processing Delay
TCP	Transmission Control Protocol
URI	Uniform Resource Identifier
URL	Uniform Resource Locator
UML	Unified Modeling Language
VCR	Video Cassette Recorder
VRML	Virtual Reality Modeling Language
WWW	World Wide Web
XML	EXtended Markup Language

Reading is to the mind what exercise is to the body.
— Sir Richard Steele

References

[Aar99]   T. Aaron. "Educational fusion: A distributed visual environment for teaching algorithms". Master's thesis, Massachusetts Institute of Technology, 1999.

[AC96]   M. Abadi and L. Cardelli. "A Theory of Objects". New York, Springer, 1996.

[ADL00]   Advanced Distributed Learning (ADL) Initiative doing their Sharable Courseware Object Reference Model (SCORM), 2000. http://www.adlnet.org

[AIS+77]   C. Alexander, S. Ishikawa, M. Silverstein, M. Jacobson, I. Fiksdahl-King, and S. Angell. "A Pattern Language". Oxford University Press, 1977.

[And96]   J.R. Anderson. "Rules of the Mind". Lawrence Erlbaum, Hillsdale, NJ, 1996.

[App95]   Apple Computer. "OpenDoc Programmer's Guide". 1995.

[ARI00]   Alliance of Remote Instructional Authoring and Distribution Networks for Europe, ARIADNE. project of European Union, 2000. http://ariadne.unil.ch

[AWFKK97]   H. Abdel-Wahab, J. Favereau, O. Kim, and P. Kabore. "An internet collaborative environment for sharing java applications". In IEEE Computer Society Workshop on Future Trends of Distributed Systems (FTDCS'97), pages 112–117, Tunis, Tunisia, October 29–31 1997.

[AWFKK98]   H. Abdel-Wahab, J. Favereau, O. Kim, and P. Kabore. "Replication management of application sharing for multimedia conferencing and collaboration". In Second IFIP/IEEE International Conference on Managing Multimedia Networks and Services, Versailles, France, November 1998.

[BCK+97]   D. Bäumer, G. Cryczan, R. Knoll, C. Lilienthal, D. Riehle, and H. Zühlinghoven. "Framework development for large systems". Communications of the ACM, 40(10), pages52–59, October 1997.

[BK91]   J. Bentley and B. Kernighan. "A system for algorithm animation". Computing Systems, 4(1), pages 5–31, 1991.

[BKZ93]   R. Banker, R. Kauffman, and D. Zweig. "Repository evaluation of software reuse". IEEE Transaction on Software Engineering, 19(4), pages 379–389, April 1993.

[BMA97]   D. Brugali, G. Menga, and A. Aarsten. "The framework life span". Communications of the ACM, 40(10), pages 65–68, October 1997.

[BMMB]   J. Bosch, P. Molin, M. Mattson, and P. Bengtson. "Object-oriented frameworks - problems & experiences". In Proceedings of the 23rd International Conference in Technology of Object-Oriented Languages and Systems, pages 203–214, TOOLS '97 USA, Santa Barbara, California, July-August 1997.
             http://www.ide.hk-r.se/ michaelm/papers/ex-frame.ps.

[BN93]   M. Brown and M. A. Najork. "Algorithm animation using 3d interactive graphics". In ACM Symp. on User Interface Software and Technology, pages 93–100, 1993.

[Boe88]   B Boehm. "A spiral model of software development and enhancement". IEEE Software, 25(5), pages 61–72, May 1988.

[Boo94]   G. Booch. "Object-Oriented Analysis and Design with Applications". The Benjamin/Cummings Publishing Company, INC., 2nd edition,
             ISBN: 0-8053-5340-2.1994.

[Boy97]   N. Boyd. "A platform for distributed learning and teachning of algorithmic concepts". Master's thesis, Massachusetts Institute of Technology, 1997.

[BRM98]   C. Burger, K. Rothermel, and R. Mecklenburg. "Interactive protocol simulation applets for distance education". In Proc. of International Workshop on Interactive Distributed Multimedia Systems and Telecommunication Services 98 (IDMS 98), pages 29–40. ISSN 0302-9743. Springer, september 1998.

[Bro88a]   M. Brown. "Exploring algorithms using BALSA-II". IEEE Computer, 21(5), pages 14–36, May 1988.

[Bro88b]   M. Brown. "Perspectives on algorithm animation". In Conference proceedings on Human factors in computing systems, pages 33–38, May 1988.

[Bro91]   M. Brown. "Zeus: A system for algorithm animation and multi-view editing". In IEEE Workshop on Visual Languages, pages 4–9, October 1991. Also appeared as SRC Research Report 75.

[BS81]   R. Baecker and D. Sherman. "Sorting out sorting". In Proceedings of ACM SIGGRAPH, Shown at SIGGRAPH '81, 16mm color sound film, Dallas, Texas, 1981.

[BS84]   M. Brown and R. Sedgewick. "A system for algorithm animation". In SIGGRAPH Proceedings, volume 18, pages 177–186, July 1984.

[BS98]   J. Begole and C. Shaffer. "Flexible collaboration transparency". Technical Report TR-98-11, Virginia Tech, Department of Computer Science, 1998.

[BSSS97]   J. Begole, C. Struble, C. Shaffer, and R. Smith. "Transparent sharing of Java applets: A replicated approach". In Proceeding of the 1997 Symposium on User Interface Software and Technology (UIST'97). ACM Press, NY, 1997.

[BZB+97]   R. Braden, L. Zhang, S. Berson, S. Herzog, and S. Jamin. "Rfc 2205–Resource Reservation Protocol (RSVP)" version 1 functional specification, September 1997.

[CBN89]   A. Collins, J.S. Brown, and S.E. Newman. "Knowing, learning, and instruction: Essays in honor of Robert Glaser", chapter Cognitive apprenticeship: Teaching the craft of reading, writing, and mathematics, pages 453– 494. Hillsdale, NJ, Erlbaum, 1989.

[CGJ+98]   A. Chabert, E. Grossman, L. Jackson, S. Pietrowiz, and C. Seguin. "Java object-sharing in Habanero". Communications of the ACM, 41(6), pages 69–76, June 1998.

[Coa92]   P. Coad. "Object-oriented patterns". Communications of the ACM, 35(9), pages 152–159, 1992.

[Cor]   Microsoft Corporation. "NetMeeting Resource Kit". Version of October 18, 2000. http://www.microsoft.com/windows/NetMeeting.

[CR92]   K. Cox and G. Roman. "Abstraction in algorithm animation". In Proceedings of the 1992 IEEE Workshop on Visual Languages, pages 18–24, Seattle, Washington, Sept. 15–18, 1992.

[CS96]   B. Childs and J. Sametinger. "Reuse measurement with line and word runs". In Proceeding of the TOOLS Pacific'96, November 1996.

[Dav96]   C. David. "Understanding ActiveX and OLE". Microsoft Press, 1996.

[DC00]   Provisional report of the Dublin Core subelement working group, 2000.
                    http://purl.oclc.org/ metadata/dublin_core/wsubelementdrafts.html

[DGO+94]   G. Dermler, T. Gutekunst, E. Ostrowski, N. Pires, T. Schmidt, M. Weber, and H. Wolf. "JVTOS – multimedia telecooperation interconnecting heterogeneous platforms". In Proceedings of International Conference on Broadband Islands, 1994.

[Dij79]   E. Dijkstra. "Programming Considered as a Human Activity". Yourdon Press, 1979.

[DM91]   J. Diederich and J. Milton. "Creating domain specific metadata for scientific data and knowledge bases". In IEEE Transactions on Knowledge and Data Engineering, volume 3, pages 421–434, December 1991.

[EDS00]   A. El Saddik, J. Diaz, and R. Steinmetz. "Customizability of Visualizations in Web-based learning systems". In Proceedings of VI Argentine Congress on Computer Science, the Congress at the End of the World, Argentina, October 2000.

[EFS99]   A. El Saddik, S. Fischer, and R. Steinmetz. "Component-based framework for effective visualization of educational algorithms". In H.-J. Bullinger, P. H. Vossen (Eds.): Adjunct Confernce Proceedings of HCI International '99. Stuttgart, Fraunhofer IRB Verlag, August 1999.

[EFS00]   A. El Saddik, S. Fischer, and R. Steinmetz. "iTBeanKit: An educational middleware framework for bridging software technology and education". In Proccedings of EdMedia 2000, Montreal, Canada, June 2000.

[EFS01]   A. El Saddik, S. Fischer, and R. Steinmetz. "Reusability and Adaptability of Interactive Resources in Web-based Educational Systems". ACM Journal of Educational Resources in Computing (JERIC), volume 1, issue 1, 2001.

[EGFS00]   A. El Saddik, A. Ghavam, S. Fischer, and R. Steinmetz. "Metadata for Smart Multimedia Learning Objects". In Proceedings of the fourth Australasian Computing Education Conference. ACM-CSE, December 2000.

[EKFS99]   A. El Saddik, O. Karaduman, S. Fischer, and R. Steinmetz. "Collaborative working with stand-alone applets". In Proc. of the 12th International Symposium on Intelligent Multimedia and Distance Education(ISIMADE'99), pages 203–209, August 1999. ISBN: 0-921836-80-5.

[Eng97]   R. Englander. "Developing JavaBeans". ISBN 1-56592-289-1. O'Reilly, first edition, 1997.

[Eoe00]   Educational object economy, 2000.
              http://www.eoe.org

[ES98]   W. Effelsberg and R. Steinmetz. "Video Compression Techniques". ISBN: 3-920993-13-6. dpunkt Verlag, 1998.

[ESGS00]   A. El Saddik, S. Shirmohammadi, N. Georganas, and R. Steinmetz. "Jasmine: Java application sharing in multiuser interactive environments". In International Workshop on Interactive Distributed Multimedia Systems and Telecommunication Services 2000 (IDMS 2000), pages 214–226. Springer, October 2000.

[ESH+97]   A. El Saddik, M. Schumacher, C. Herzog, O. Groehn, P. Ilboudo, and R. Steinmetz. "Java in der interaktiven lehre". In Proceedings of the Workshop on Java in Telecommunications May 1997, may 1997. ITG FA 6.2 System- und Anwendungssoftware Deutsche Telekom.

[ESS+99]   A. El Saddik, C. Seeberg, A. Steinacker, K. Reichenberger, S. Fischer, and R. Steinmetz. "A component-based construction kit for algorithmic visualizations". In Proceedings of the Integrated Design & Process technology (IDPT'99), ISSN 1090-9389, page 40 (full version on CD). June 1999.

[Eth00]   ANSI/IEEE standard IEEE-802.3, Ethernet, 2000.

[Fdi96]   S. Fdida. "High-Speed Networking for Multimedia Applications", chapter Multimedia Transport Protocol and Multicast Communication. Kluwer Academic Publishers, Boston/Dordrecht/London, 1996.

[FE99]   S. Fischer and A. El Saddik. "Open Java: Von den Grundlagen zu den Anwendungen". ISBN: 3-540 65446-1. Springer, 1999.

[FEH+00]   A. Faatz, A. El Saddik, S. Hörmann, I. Rimac, C. Seeberg, A. Steinacker, and R. Steinmetz. "Multimedia und Wissen: Unser Weg zu einem produktiven Umgang mit Wissensdurst". Thema Forschung, 2, November 2000.

[Fre97]   M. Freeman. "Flexibility in access, interaction and assessment: The case for web-based teaching programs". Australian Journal of Educational Technology, 13(1), pages 23–39, 1997.

[FS97]   M. Fayad and D. Schmidt. "Object-oriented application frameworks". Communications of the ACM, 40(10), pages 32–38, October 1997.

[FS00]   S. Fischer and R. Steinmetz. "Automatic Creation of Exercises in Adaptive Hypermedia Learning Systems". In Proceedings of 11th ACM Conference on Hypertext and Hypermedia (HT00). ACM, June 2000.

[GEM00]   The Gateway to Educational Materials (GEM), 2000.
              http://www.geminfo.org

[Geo00]	N. Georganas. "Distributed Virtual Environments for Training and Telecollaboration". In Proceedings of IEEE Instrumentation and Measurement Technology Conference (IMTC'99). Venice, Italy, May 1999.
[GG95]	K. Green and S. Gilbert. "Great expectations: Content, communications, productivity, and the role of information technology in higher education". Change, 27(2), pages 8–19, March-April 1995.
[GHJV97]	E. Gamma, R. Helm, R. Johnson, and J. Vlissides. "Design Patterns: Elements of Reusable Object-Oriented Software". ISBN: 0-201-63361-2. Addison Wesley, 1997.
[Glo]	Instruktion und Interaktive Medien (iim) arbeitsgruppe prof. ulrich glowalla am fachbereich psychologie der universität gießen. http://paedglo.psychol.uni-giessen.de/
[Glo97]	P. Gloor. "Elements of Hypermedia Design: Techniques for Navigation & Visualization in Cyberspace". ISBN: 0-8176-3911. Birkhäuser, 1997.
[Glo98]	P. Gloor. "Software Visualization", chapter User Interface Issues for Algorithm Animation, pages 145–152. ISBN: 0-262-19395-7. MIT Press, 1998.
[GR89]	A. Goldberg and D. Robson. "Smalltalk-80: The Language". Addison Wesley, 1989.
[Gro00]	IEEE Learning Technology Standards Committee (LTSC) IEEE P1484.12 Learning Objects Metadata Working Group, 2000. http://ltsc.ieee.org/wg12/, 2000.
[GS88]	G. Grasner and S. Pope. "A cookbook for using the model-view-controller user interface paradigm in smaltalk-80". Object Orinted Programming, 1(3), 1988.
[GSvD99]	D. Gould, R. Simpson, and A. van Dam. "Granularity in the design of interactive illustrations". In ACM SIGCSE, New Orleans, L.A., 1999.
[GWY94]	D. Garfinkel, B. Welti, and T. Yip. "HP SharedX: A tool for real-time collaboration". Hewlett-Packard Journal, pages 23–26, April 1994.
[HDP92]	W. Hibbard, C. Dyer, and B. Paul. "Display of scientific data structures for algorithm visualization". In Proceedings of IEEE Visualization '92, pages 139–146, 1992.
[Hep00]	D. Hepting. "Mathematical visualization resources", 2000. http://fas.sfu.ca/~dhepting/personal/research/math-viz.

[HM98]   F. Howell and R. McNab. "SimJava: a discrete event simulation package for Java with applications in computer systems modeling". In Proceedings of the First International Conference on Web-based Modeling and Simulation, San Diego, CA, January 1998.

[HNS98]   S. Hansen, N.. Narayanan, and D. Schrimpsher. "Rethinking algorithm animation: A framework for effective visualizations". In Proceedings of the World Conference on Educational Multimedia and Hypermedia (ED-MEDIA'98), 1998.

[Hof95]   N. Hoft. "International Technical Communication: How to Export Information About High Technology". Wiley: New York, NY, 1995.

[Hol00]   S. Holzner. "Inside XML". Number ISBN: 0735710201. New Riders Publishing, 1st edition, 2000.

[Hop00]   J. Hopkins. "Component Primer". Communications of the ACM, 43(10), pages 27–30, October 2000.

[HP98]   H.. Hege and K. Polthier (eds.). "Mathematical Visualization - Algorithms, Applications, and Numerics". ISBN: 3-540-63991-8. Springer, 1998.

[HPS+94]   W. Hibbard, B. Paul, D. Santek, C. Dyer, A. Battaiola, and M. Voidrot-Martinez. "Interactive visualization of earth and space science computations". IEEE Computer, 27(7), pages 65–72, July 1994.

[HSN98]   S. Hansen, D. Schrimpsher, and N. . Narayanan. "Learning algorithms by visualization: A novel approach using animation-embedded hypermedia". In Proceedings of the Third International Conference on The Learning Sciences, pages 125–130. Association for the Advancement of Computing in Education, 1998.

[IMS00]   Educom's Instructional Management Systems project (IMS), 2000. http://www.imsproject.org

[Inc95]   Multimedia Communication Forum Inc. "Multimedia communication quality of service", September 24 1995. Approved Rev 1.0.

[inf00]   InfoQuilt: "Information brokering for globally distributed heterogenous digital media". Large Scale Distributed Information Systems Lab, Department of Computer Science, University of Georgia, 2000.
            http://lsdis.cs.uga.edu/infoquilt

[IPOLD00]   On-Line Dictionary, Internet Encyclopedia, & Almanac Reference, 2000.
            http://www.infoplease.com/ipd/A0728467.html

[JI00]   Sun JavaSoft. "InfoBus", 2000.
            http://java.sun.com/products/javabeans/infobus/index.html

[Jav00]   Sun javasoft web site, 2000.
http://java.sun.com

[JDE92]   B. Price J. Domingue and M. Eisenstadt. "A framework for describing and implementing software visualization systems". In Proceedings of Graphics Interface '92, pages 53–60, May 1992.

[JF88]   R. Johnson and B. Foote. "Designing reusable classes". The Journal of Object-Oriented Programming, 1(2), pages 22–35, 1988.
ftp://st.cs.uiuc.edu/pub/papers/frameworks/designing-reusable-classes.ps.

[Joh99]   Mark Johnson. "Bean markup language". Java World, October 1999.

[JR91]   R. Johnson and V. Russo. "Reusing object oriented design". Technical report, University of Illinois, , 1991.
ftp://st.cs.uiuc.edu/pub/papers/frameworks/reusable-oo-design.ps.

[Kam99]   T. Kamps. "Diagram Design: A Constructive Theory". ISBN: 3-540-65439-9 Springer-Verlag, 1999.

[KBKT99]   M. Koutis, G. Birbilis, K. Kynigos, and G. Tsironis. "E-slate: a kit of educational components". In Proceedings of AI-ED '99 International Conference, LeMans, France, 1999.

[KfFK96]   M. Kuhn, f. Findeiss, and N. Klinnert. "Jugend und Neue Medien". Chapter: Formen des Lernens am Computer. A-L-F Verlag Nuerenberg, 1996.

[KFS98]   C. Kuhmnuech, T. Fuhrmann, and G. Schæppe. "Java teachware - the Java remote control tool and its applications". In procceding of ED-MEDIA'98, 1998.

[KH98]   R. Klein and F. Hanisch. "Using a modular construction kit for the realization of an interactive computer graphics course". In EdMedia'1998. Association for the Advancement of Computing in Education (AACE), USA, 1998.

[Kos96]   T. Koshmann. "Theory and Practice of an Emerging Paradigm". Lawrence Erlbaum, Mahwah, NJ, 1996.

[Kru92]   C. Krueger. "Software reuse". ACM Computing Surveys, 24, June 1992.

[Lag]   Carl Lagoze. "The warwick framework, a container architecture for diverse sets of metadata". d-lib magazine, july/august 1996.
http://www.dlib.org/dlib/july96/lagoze/07lagoze.html

[LF]   L.Rostek and D. Fischer. "SFK: A Smalltalk Frame Kit, Concepts and Use" (Draft).
http://www.darmstadt.gmd.de/ rostek/sfkman3.1/index.html

[LJTD95]	T. Luong, J. Lok, D. Taylor, and K. Driscoll. "Internationalization: Developing Software for Global Markets". Wiley: New York, NY, 1995.
[Mat96]	M. Mattsson. "Object Oriented Frameworks: Asurvey of methodological issues". Technical report, University of Karlskrona/Ronneby, Sweden, 1996.
[MPFL97]	J. Mitchell, W. Pennebaker, C. Fogg, and D. LeGall. "MPEG video compression standard". ISBN: 0-412-08771-5. Chapman &Hall, 1997.
[MPG98]	A. Blackwell, M. Petre and T. Green. "Software Visualization", chapter Cognitive Questions in Software Visualization. ISBN: 0-262-19395-7. MIT Press, 1998.
[MT87]	W. Mann and S. Thomson. "Rhetorical structure theory: A theory of text organization". Technical Report RS-87-190, Information Science Institute, USC ISI, 1987.
[Mul00]	The multibook project homepage, 2000. http://www.multibook.de
[Mye90]	B. Myer. "Taxonomies of visual programming and program visualization". Visual Languages and Computating, (1), pages 97–123, March 1990.
[Nap90]	T. Naps. "Algorithm visualization in computer science laboratories". In Proceedings of the 21st SIGCSE Technical Symposium on Computer Science Education, pages 105–110, Washington DC., February 1990.
[Nap96]	T. Naps. "Algorithm visualization served off the world wide web: why and how". In Proceedings of the conference on Integrating technology into computer science education, pages 192–200, Barcelona Spain, June 1996.
[NS99]	C North and B. Shneiderman. "Snap-together visualization: Evaluating coordination usage and construction". Technical Report 99-26, University of Maryland, Human Computer Interaction Lab, October 1999.
[Obr98]	K. Obraczka. "Multicast transport protcols: A survey and taxonomy". IEEE Communications, 36(1), pages 94–102, 1998.
[oC00]	Free On-Line Dictionary of Computing, 2000. http://foldoc.doc.ic.ac.uk/foldoc/index.html
[OH98]	R. Orfali and D. Harkey. "Client/Server Programming with Java and CORBA". New York: John Wiley and Sons, 1998.
[O'N98]	J. O'Neil. "JavaBeans Programming from the Ground Up". ISBN: 0-07-882477-x. Osborne, 1998.

[Opd92]	W. Opdyke. "Refactoring Object-Oriented Frameworks". PhD thesis, University of Illinois at Urbana-Champaign, ftp://st.cs.uiuc.edu/pub/papers/refactoring/opdyke-thesis.ps.Z, 1992.
[Ora98]	L Ora. "Web metadata: a matter of semantics". In IEEE Internet Computing, number 4, pages 30–37, July, August 1998.
[Pal]	Richard S. Palais. "What Is Mathematical Visualization?" http://rsp.math.brandeis.edu/3D-Filmstrip_html/Documentation/DocumentationPages/WhatIsMathViz.html
[Par00]	The paradelektion homepage (iTBeanKit project), 2000. http://www.kom.e-technik.tu-darmstadt.de/projects/iteach/itbean-kit/html/
[PD89]	R. Prieto-Diaz. "Software Reusability: Concepts and Models". Volume 1 of Frontier Series, chapter Classification od Reusable Modules. ACM Press, 1989.
[PED+99]	N. Poerwantoro, A. El Saddik, T. Dammann, S. Fischer, B. Krämer, and R. Steinmetz. "A component-based model for interactive tests". In Workshop im Rahmen der 29. Jahrestagung der Gesellschaft für Informatik (Informatik 99), october 1999. HNF Heinz Nixdorf MuseumsForum, Paderborn.
[PEKS00]	N. Poerwantoro, A. El Saddik, B. Krämer, and R. Steinmetz. "Multibook's test environment". In Proccedings of the 22nd. International Conference on Software Engineering (ICSE2000), pages 680–684, june June 4 -11 2000. Limerick, Ireland.
[PLV97]	E. Posnak, G. Lavender, and H. Vin. "An adaptive framework for developing multimedia software components". Communications of the ACM, 40(10), pages 43–47, October 1997.
[Pou97]	J. Poulin. "Measuring Software Reuse: Principles, Practices and Economic Models". Addison-Wesley, 1997.
[Pre95]	W. Pree. "Design Patterns for Object-Oriented Software development". Addison-Wesley, 1995.
[PS95]	J. Preece and B. Shneiderman. "Survival of the fittest: The evolution of multimedia user interfaces". ACM Computing Surveys, 27(4), pages 558–559, December 1995.
[PSS93]	B Price, R Small, and I. Small. "A principled taxonomy of software visualization". Visual Languages and Computing, 4(3), pages 211–266, September 1993.
[Qua99]	T. Quatrani. "Visual Modelling with Rational Rose and UML". ISBN: 0-201-31016-3. Addison-Wesley, 1999.

[RDF00]	Resource Description Framework (RDF), 2000. http://www.w3.org/RDF/
[RDK+99]	J. Roschelle, C. DiGiano, M. Koutlis, A. Repenning, J. Phillips, N. Jackiw, and D. Suthers. "Developing educational software components". IEEE Computer, 32(9), pages 50–58, September 1999.
[RER98]	A. Rose, D. Eckard, and G. Rubloff. "An application framework for creating simulation-based learing environments". Technical Report 98-07, University of Maryland, Human Computer Interaction Lab, May 1998.
[RJB99]	J. Rumbaugh, I. Jacobson, and G. Booch. "The Unified Modeling Language Rafereance Manual". ISBN: 0-201-30998-x. Addison-Wesley, 1999.
[Sam97]	J. Sametinger. "Software Engineering with Reusable Components". ISBN: 3-540-62695-6. Springer Verlag, 1997.
[SBL93]	J. Stasko, A. Badro, and C. Lewis. "Do algorithm animations assist learning? an empirical study and analysis". In Proceedings of the conference on Human factors in computing systems, pages 61–66, 1993.
[See01]	C Seeberg. "Adaptivität in webbasierten Multimedia-Lernsystemen mit modularer Wissensbasis". Darmstadt University of Technology. 2001
[SEGS01a]	S. Shirmohammadi, A. El Saddik, N. Georganas, and R. Steinmetz. "JASMINE: A Java Tool for Multimedia Collaboration on the Internet". Journal of Multimedia Tools and Applications. Kluwer Academic Publishers, to appear.
[SEGS01b]	S. Shirmohammadi, A. El Saddik, N.. Georganas, and R. Steinmetz. "Web-Based Multimedia Tools for Sharing Educational Resources". ACM Journal of Educational Resources in Computing (JERIC), volume 1, issue 1, 2001.
[SER+98]	C. Seeberg, A. El Saddik, K. Reichenberger, A. Steinacker, S. Fischer, and R. Steinmetz. "iTeach - interactive teaching and learning". ISBN: 1-58113-036-8 Description of the Multibook Demo, Contribution to the ACM MM in the category "Technical Demo". September 1998.
[SF97]	D. Schmidt and M. Fayad. "Lessons learned, building reusable object-oriented frameworks for distributed software". Communications of the ACM, 40(10), pages 85–87, October 1997.
[SFC94]	M. Storey, F. Fracchia, and S. Carpendale. "A top-down approach to algorithm animation". Technical Report Techical Report CMPT 94-05, School of Computing Science, Simon Fraser University, Burnaby, B.C., CANADA, 1994.

[SG78]	S. Shirmohammadi and N. D. Georganas. "JETS: a Java-Enabled Telecollaboration System". In IEEE Conference on Multimedia Computing and Systems (ICMCS '97), 19978.
[SGS01]	A. Steinacker, A. Ghavam, and R. Steinmetz. "Metadata Standards for Web-based Resources". IEEE Multimedia, Vol 8(1) pp.70–76, January 2001.
[SHE00]	C. Schremmer, V. Hilt and W. Effelsberg. "Erfahrungen mit synchronen und asynchronen Lernszenarien an der Universität Mannheim". Praxis in der Informationsverarbeitung und Kommunikation (PIK), 1(03/00), pages 121–128, 2000.
[Shn96]	B. Shneiderman. "The eyes have it: A task by data type taxonomy for information visualizations". In Proceedings Visual Languages 96. University of Maryland, Human Computer Interaction Lab, September 1996.
[Shn97]	B Shneiderman. "Codex, memex, genex: The pursuit of transformational technologies". In International Journal of Human-Computer Interaction, December 1997.
[Sim99]	R. Sims. "Interactivity on stage: Strategies for learner-designer communication". In Australian Journal of Educational Technology, 15(3), pages 257–272, 1999.
[SL98]	J. Stasko and A. Lawrence. "Software Visualization", chapter Empirically Assessing Algorithm Animations as Learning Aids. ISBN: 0-262-19395-7. MIT Press, 1998.
[SM99]	Inc. Sun Microsystems. "Java Look and Feel Design Guidelines". Addison-Wesley, 1999.
[SN95]	R. Steinmetz and K. Nahrstedt. "Multimedia computing, communications, and applications". ISBN: 0-13-324435-0. Prentice Hall, 1995.
[SOG98]	S. Shirmohammadi, J. C. Oliveira, and N. D. Georganas. "Java-based multimedia collaboration: Approaches and issues". In International Conference On Telecommunications (ICT '98), volume I, Porto Carras, Greece, 1998.
[Som00]	I. Sommerville. "Software Engineering". ISBN: 0-201-39815-x. Addison-Wesley, 6th edition, 2000.
[Sow91]	J. Sowa. "Principles of Semantic Networks: Explorations in the Representation of Knowledge", chapter Toward the Expressive Power of Natural Language, pages 157–189. Morgan Kaufmann, San Mateo, CA, 1991.
[Spa00]	M. Sparling. "Lessons learned through six years of component-based development". Communications of the ACM, 43(10), pages 47–53, October 2000.

[SRH+00]   C. Seeberg, I. Rimac, S. Hörmann, A. Faatz, A. Steinacker and A. El Saddik, and R. Steinmetz. "MediBook: Realisierung eines generischen Ansatzes für ein interentbasiertes Multimedia-Lernsystem am Beispiel Medizin". In Tagungsband: Treffen der GI-Fachgruppe 1.1.3 Maschinelles Lernen (GMD Report 114), pages 96–105, September 2000.

[SRH+01]   A. Steinacker, I. Rimac, S. Hörmann, A. Faatz, C. Seeberg, A. El Saddik, and R. Steinmetz. "Medibook: Combining semantic networks with metadata for learning resources to build a web based learning system". in EdMedia'2001, Tampere, Finland, June 2001.

[SS01]   Bertelsmann Stifftung and Heinz Nixdorf Stifftung, (eds.). "Evalis: Evaluation Interaktiven Studierens. Studierverhalten in Präsenzveranstaltungen und Online-Bildungsangeboten". Bertelsmann Foundation Publisher, 2001.

[SSFS99]   A. Steinacker, C. Seeberg, S. Fischer, and R. Steinmetz. "Multibook: Metadata for the web". In Proceedings of the 2nd International Conference on New Learning Technologies, pages 16–24, Bern, Swizzerland, 1999.

[SSR+99a]   C. Seeberg, A. Steinacker, K. Reichenberger, A. El Saddik, S. Fischer, and R. Steinmetz. "From the user's needs to adaptive documents". In Proceedings of the IDPT, ISSN 1090-9389, page 30 (full paper on CD), June 1999.

[SSR+99b]   C. Seeberg, A. Steinacker, K. Reichenberger, S. Fischer, and R. Steinmetz. "Individual tables of contents in web-based learning systems". In Proceedings of the 10th ACM Conference on Hypertext and Hypermedia, pages 167–168, 1999.

[SSR+99c]   A. Steinacker, C. Seeberg, K. Reichenberger, S. Fischer, and R. Steinmetz. "Dynamically Generated Tables of Contents as Guided Tours in Adaptive Hypermedia Systems". In Proceedings of the EdMedia & EdTelecom, pages 167–175, June 1999. ISBN: 1-58113-064-3.

[SSS00a]   J. Schümmer, T. Schümmer, and C. Schuckmann. "COAST-ein anwendungsframework für synchrone groupware". In Proceedings of Net.ObjectDays 2000, pages 288 – 299, Erfurt, Germany, October 2000.

[SSS00b]   A. Steinacker, C. Seeberg, and R. Steinmetz. "Coherence in modularly composed adaptive learning documents". In Proceedings of Adaptive Hypermedia AH2000, ISBN: 3-540-67910-3, pages 375–379. Springer-Verlag, 2000.

[SSvD99]   R. Simpson, A. Spalter, and A. van Dam. "Exploratories: An educational strategy for the 21st century". In Proceedings of SIGGRAPH '99 Educational Schoolhouse Lecture, 1999.

[Sta90a]   J. Stasko. "The path transition paradigm: a practical methodology for adding animation to program interfaces". Visual Languages and Computing, 1(3), pages 213–236, 1990.

[Sta90b]   J. Stasko. "Tango: A framework and system for algorithm animation". IEEE Computer, 23(9), pages 27–39, September 1990.

[Sta92]   J. Stasko. "Animating algorithms with Xtango". In SIGACT News (ACM Special Interest Group on Automata and Computability Theory), volume 23, pages 67–71, 1992.

[Ste00]   R. Steinmetz. "Multimedia-Technologie: Grundlagen, Komponenten und Systeme". Springer-Verlag, October 2000. 3. Auflage (erstmalig mit CD).

[Ste98]   R. Steinmetz. "Multimedia-Technologie: Grundlagen, Komponenten und Systeme". Springer-Verlag, October 1998. 2. Auflage.

[Szy97]   C. Szyperski. "Component Software: Beyond Object-Oriented Programming". ISBN: 0-201-17888-5. ACM-PRESS, Addison-Wesley, 1997.

[tal96]   Taligent White Papers, "Leveraging Object-Oriented Frameworks - A Technology Primer from Taligent", 1996.
                http://www.ibm.com/java/education/ooleveraging/index.html.

[Tan96]   A. Tannenbaum. "Computer Networks". Prentice Hall, 1996. 3rd Ed.

[Tay80]   R. Taylor, (ed.). "The Computer in the School: Tutor, Tool, Tutee". ASIN: 0807726117. New York: Teachers College Press, 1980.

[TD95]   A. Tal and D. Dobkin. "Visualization of geometric algorithms". IEEE Transactions on Visualization and Computer Graphics (TVCG), 1(2), 1995.

[tedoctc00]   Technical Encyclopedia: definitions of computer terms and concepts, 2000.
                http://www.techweb.com/encyclopedia

[TS00]   D. Tietze and R. Steinmetz. "Verteiltes Arbeiten - Arbeit der Zukunft". In R. Reichwald and J. Schlichter, (eds), Proceedings der Fachtagung D-CSCW 2000, ISBN: 3-519-02695-3, pages 49–62. German Chapter of the ACM, Berichte, 54, Stuttgart, B.G.Teubner, September 2000.

[TSDT00]   Java Shared Data Toolkit, 2000
                http://www.sun.com/ software/jsdt/index.html

[WHRT01]   W. Wang, J. Haake, J. Rubart, D. Tietze. "Hypermedia-based Support for Cooperative Learning of Process Knowledge". In: Journal of Network and Computer Applications, Vol. 23, pp. 357-379, Academic Press, 2001.

[Wil00]   J. Wilcox. "Videoconferencing & Interactive Multimedia: The Whole Picture". Telecom Books, New York. ISBN: 1-57820-054-7. 2000

[Wir90]   N. Wirth. "Modula-2 and object oriented programming". Microprocessors and Microsystems, 14(3), pages 148–152, apr 1990.

[WR92]   N. Wirth and M. Reiser. "Programming in Oberon - Steps Beyond Pascal and Modula". ISBN: 0-201-56543-9. Addison-Wesley, first edition, 1992.

I have always grown from my problems and challenges
from the things that don't work out
that's when I've really learned

Author's Publications

Books

[FE99]   Stephan Fischer and Abdulmotaleb El Saddik. "Open Java: Von den Grundlagen zu den Anwendungen". ISBN: 3-540 65446-1. Springer, 1999.

[LLE00]   George E. Lasker, Sheng-Tun Li and Abdulmotaleb El Saddik (Eds). "Proceedings of the 2nd International Workshop on Advances in Software Engineering and Multimedia Applications (SEMA 2000)". Published by The International Institute For Advanced Studies In Systems Research And Cybernetics, August 2000.

Journals

[EFS01]   Abdulmotaleb El Saddik, Stephan Fischer, and Ralf Steinmetz. "Reusability and Adaptability of Interactive Resources in Web-based Educational Systems". ACM Journal of Educational Resources in Computing (JERIC), volume 1, issue 1, 2001.

[ES01]   Adulmotaleb El Saddik and Ralf Steinmetz. "Ein Java-basiertes Werkzeug für transparente Kollaboration über das Internet". Thema Forschung, 1, ISSN 1434-7468, pages 56-61, March 2001.

[FEH+00]   Andreas Faatz, Adulmotaleb El Saddik, Stefan Hörmann, Ivica Rimac, Cornelia Seeberg, Achim Steinacker, and Ralf Steinmetz. "Multimedia und Wissen: Unser Weg zu einem produktiven Umgang mit Wissensdurst". Thema Forschung, 2, ISSN 1434-7768, November 2000.

[SEGS01a] Shervin Shirmohammadi, Abdulmotaleb El Saddik, Nicolas D. Georganas, and Ralf Steinmetz. "Web-Based Multimedia Tools for Sharing Educational Resources". ACM Journal of Educational Resources in Computing (JERIC), volume 1, issue 1, 2001.

[SEGS01b]   Shervin Shirmohammadi, Abdulmotaleb El Saddik, Nicolas D. Georganas, and Ralf Steinmetz. "JASMINE: A Java Tool for Multimedia Collaboration on the Internet". Journal of Multimedia Tools and Applications, Kluwer Academic Publishers, to appear.

Conference Proceedings and Workshops

[DAE+00]   Vasilios Darlagiannis, Ralf Ackermann, Abdulmotaleb El Saddik, Nicolas Georganas, and Ralf Steinmetz. "Suitability of java for virtual collaboration". In Proc. of Net ObjectDays 2000, Erfurt Germany, pages 71-78, October 2000.

[EDS00]   Abdulmotaleb El Saddik, Javier Diaz, and Ralf Steinmetz. "Customizability of Visualizations in Web-based learning systems". In Proceedings of VI Argentine Congress on Computer Science, the Congress at the End of the World, October 2000.

[EFS99]   Abdulmotaleb El Saddik, Stephan Fischer, and Ralf Steinmetz. "Component-based framework for effective visualization of educational algorithms". In H.-J. Bullinger, P. H. Vossen (Eds.): Adjunct Confernce Proceedings of HCI International '99. Stuttgart:Fraunhofer IRB Verlag, August 1999.

[EFS00]   Abdulmotaleb El Saddik, Stephan Fischer, and Ralf Steinmetz. "iT-BeanKit: An educational middleware framework for bridging software technology and education". In Proccedings of EdMedia 2000, Montreal, Canada, June 2000.

[EGFS00]   Abdulmotaleb El Saddik, Amir Ghavam, Stephan Fischer, and Ralf Steinmetz. "Metadata for Smart Multimedia Learning Objects". In Proceedings of the fourth Australasian Computing Education Conference. ACM-CSE, December 2000.

[EGS98]   Abdulmotaleb El Saddik, Carsten Griwodz, and Ralf Steinmetz. "Exploiting User Behaviour in Prefetching WWW Documents". In Proc. of International Workshop on Interactive Distributed Multimedia Systems and Telecommunication Services 98 (IDMS 98), pages 302–311. Springer, September 1998. ISSN 0302-9743.

[EKFS99]   Abdulmotaleb El Saddik, Oguzhan Karaduman, Stephan Fischer, and Ralf Steinmetz. "Collaborative working with stand-alone applets". In Proc. of the 12th International Symposium on Intelligent Multimedia and Distance Education(ISIMADE'99), pages 203–209, August 1999. ISBN: 0-921836-80-5.

[ESGS00]   Abdulmotaleb El Saddik, Shervin Shirmohammadi, Nicolas D. Georganas, and Ralf Steinmetz. "JASMINE: Java Application Sharing in Multiuser INteractive Environments". In International Workshop on Interactive Distributed Multimedia Systems and Telecommunication Services 2000 (IDMS 2000), pages 214–226. Springer, October 2000.

[ES01]   Abdulmotaleb El Saddik, and Ralf Steinmetz. "Keep It Simple and Smart". In Proceedings of the ACS/IEEE International Conference on Computer Systems and Applications. Beirut, Lebanon, June, 2001.

[ESH+97]   Abdulmotaleb El Saddik, Markus Schumacher, Christian Herzog, Olav Groehn, Pascal Ilboudo, and Ralf Steinmetz. "Java in der interaktiven Lehre". In Proceedings of the Workshop on Java in Telecommunications May 1997. ITG FA 6.2 System- und Anwendungssoftware Deutsche Telekom.

[ESS+99]   Abdulmotaleb El Saddik, Cornelia Seeberg, Achim Steinacker, Klaus Reichenberger, Stephan Fischer, and Ralf Steinmetz. "A component-based Construction Kit for Algorithmic Visualizations". In Proceedings of the Integrated Design & Process technology (IDPT'99), ISSN 1090-9389, page 41 (full paper on CD), June 1999.

[EWS+97]   Abdulmotaleb El Saddik, Gunter Weiss, Heiko Straulino, Utz Roedig, and Ralf Steinmetz. "Erfahrungen in der kooperativen Java-Entwicklung: Ein Praxisbericht". In Proceedings of the Workshop on Java in Telecommunications May 1997. ITG FA 6.2 System- und Anwendungssoftware Deutsche Telekom.

[GLE+01]   Carsten Griwodz, Michael Liepert, Abdulmotaleb El Saddik, Giwon On and Michael Zink. "Perceived Consistency". In Proceedings of the ACS/IEEE International Conference on Computer Systems and Applications. Beirut, Lebanon, June, 2001.

[PED+99]   Nathalie Poerwantoro, Abdulmotaleb El Saddik, Thomas Dammann, Stephan Fischer, Bernd Krämer, and Ralf Steinmetz. "A component-based Model for Interactive Tests". In Workshop im Rahmen der 29. Jahrestagung der Gesellschaft für Informatik (Informatik 99), october 1999. HNF Heinz Nixdorf MuseumsForum, Paderborn.

[PEKS00]   Nathalie Poerwantoro, Abdulmotaleb El Saddik, Bernd Krämer, and Ralf Steinmetz. "Multibook's test environment". In Proccedings of the 22nd. International Conference on Software Engineering (ICSE2000), pages 680–684, June 4 -11 2000. Limerick, Ireland.

[SER+98]   Cornelia Seeberg, Abdulmotaleb El Saddik, Klaus Reichenberger, Achim Steinacker, Stephan Fischer, and Ralf Steinmetz. "iTeach - Interactive Teaching and Learning". ISBN: 1-58113-036-8 Description of the Multibook Demo, Contribution to the ACM MM in the category "Technical Demo", September 1998.

[SFS+01]   Achim Steinacker, Andreas Faatz, Cornelia Seeberg, Ivica Rimac, Stefan Hörmann, Abdulmotaleb El Saddik and Ralf Steinmetz: "MediBook: Combining semantic networks with metadata for learning resources to build a web based learning system". In Proccedings of EdMedia 2001, Tampere, Finnland, June 2001.

[SRH+00]   Cornelia Seeberg, Ivica Rimac, Stefan Hörmann, Andreas Faatz, Achim Steinacker ans Abdulmotaleb El Saddik, and Ralf Steinmetz. "MediBook: Realisierung eines generischen Ansatzes für ein interentbasiertes Multimedia-Lernsystem am Beispiel Medizin". In Tagungsband: Treffen der GI-Fachgruppe 1.1.3 Maschinelles Lernen (GMD Report 114), pages 96–105, September 2000.

[SRH+01]   Achim Steinacker, Ivica Rimac, Stefan Hörmann, Andreas Faatz, Cornelia Seeberg, Abdulmotaleb El Saddik, and Ralf Steinmetz. "Medibook: Combining Semantic Networks with Metadata for Learning Resources to Build a Web-based Learning System". Ed-Media'2001, Tampere, Finland, June 2001.

[SSR+99]   Cornelia Seeberg, Achim Steinacker, Klaus Reichenberger, Abdulmotaleb El Saddik, Stephan Fischer, and Ralf Steinmetz. "From the user's needs to adaptive documents". In Proceedings of the IDPT, ISSN 1090-9389, page 30 (full paper on CD), June 1999.

Appendix A. Case Study: Visualization of JPEG

A.1 Fundamentals

In this section we demonstrate the use of our toolkit for multimedia algorithms. As an example we present the visualization of the different steps of the JPEG compression, including the procedures being executed at the encoder as well as those of the decoder [Ste00]. A JPEG encoder performs a series of transformations on raw image data to produce a compressed output stream, which is then transmitted to a JPEG decoder that executes these transformations in the inverse order to decompress the image. Figure 53 outlines the steps of the JPEG compression/decompression process.

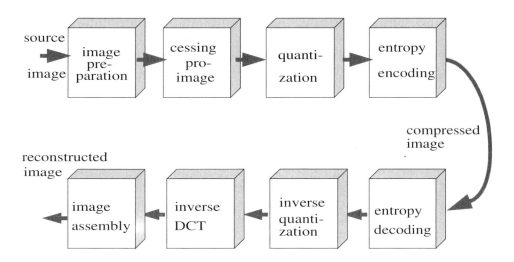

Figure 53: The JPEG Compression/decompression process

JPEG deals with colors in the YUV color space. For each separate color component (Y, U and V), the image is divided into 8x8 pixel blocks of picture elements. Each block is then transformed into a two dimensional DCT matrix. Figure 54 shows an 8x8 coefficient matrix generated by the DCT step. Coefficients with lower frequencies (typically higher values) are encoded first, followed by higher frequencies (with typically small values, near to zero).

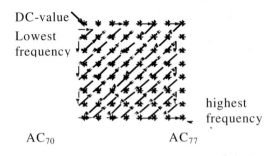

DC-value

Lowest
frequency

highest
frequency

AC_{70} AC_{77}

Figure 54: DCT processing order

The coefficients of the DCT matrix are then quantized. The final step of the JPEG compression consists of an entropy coding.

To develop an applet explaining the JPEG encoding and decoding process, a set of reusable itBeans that perform these transformations are composed as illustrated in Figure 55. The iTBeanKit library uses a fine grained modular decomposition to effectively de-couple the visualization of each step of the algorithm. This concept allows for a significant reuse of code when developing new components, and moreover some of these can directly be reused to compose other software components.

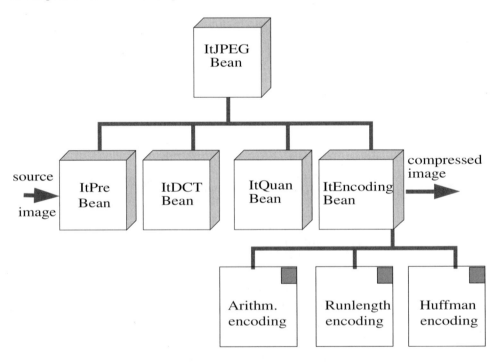

Figure 55: Components of JPEG compression process

Although, the identification of the components necessary to visualize a complex algorithm is performed applying a top-down technique, the development of these components (ItBeans) follows a bottom-up design. The development of the ItEncodingBean serves as a good example how this is achieved: no new code visualizing the encoding process has to be developed. Instead of implementing a new component, the functionality of one of the different encoding algorithms can be reused.

Each of our itBeans can have more than one view with respect to the specific needs of the user. An end-user who does not need to be concerned with the details of the DCT transformation algorithm or the Huffman encoding, but who is only interested in the general functionality of JPEG, will get the ItJPEG-Bean presenting the input and the output image with some additional information like the file size before and after the compression. Another end-user who might be interested in the execution of the DCT transformation algorithm will get the ItBeans which are located at the second level with regard to our hierarchy.

A.2 Implementation

In the following we will explain our JPEG implementation with all the necessary steps according to our framework. In order to develop an applet explaining the JPEG encoding and decoding process, a set of reusable itBeans that perform these transformations are composed as illustrated in Figure 56.

As mentioned earlier the iTBeanKit library uses a fine grained modular decomposition to effectively decouple the visualization of each algorithm. This allows a significant reuse of code when developing new components, and moreover some of these components can directly be reused to compose other software components.

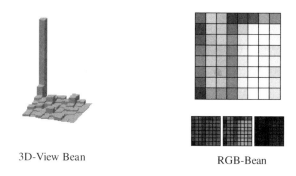

3D-View Bean   RGB-Bean

Figure 56: 3D view-Bean and RGB-Bean

The 3D view-Bean which shows the values of the Discrete Cosine Transformation, as well as the RGB-Bean, which is shown in Figure 56 are used in different applets (for example JPEG, DCT and the preparation unit applet) as to be see next.

A.2.1 JPEG

This applet visualises the JPEG compression process. As illustrated in the figure bellow, a user can choose a block on the original image on the left. When he changes the quality of the image he wants to be transmitted, the reconstructed image on the right will change according to the quality factor the user's choice. This is not the only feature of this applet. Users can also specify, whether they want the data be computed using Discrete Cosine Transformation (DCT) or Fast-DCT. They can also change the parameter of the formula if they wish. This aplet is set up out of different components. some of them are visible (3D-View, Block-chooser) and some are invisible (the data model of Run-length encoding).

The user can choose an image block and see the composition of the block in RGB (Red-Green-Blue) colors. The user can also explore the quality of the picture by choosing a higher quantization value which then decreases the quality of the picture by increasing the compression factor and decreasing the file size of the picture. If the user presses the forward button, an illustration of the steps of JPEG will be provided. By clicking on such a component a new applet window is opened and the detailed step is explained. Figure 57 illustrates the DCT visualization, having clicked on the DCT Button. As illustrated the user can switch between FDCT (Fast Discrete Cosine Transformation) and DCT (Discrete Cosine Transformation), to explore the time differences necessary to calculate the output values (DCT is outperformed by FDCT).

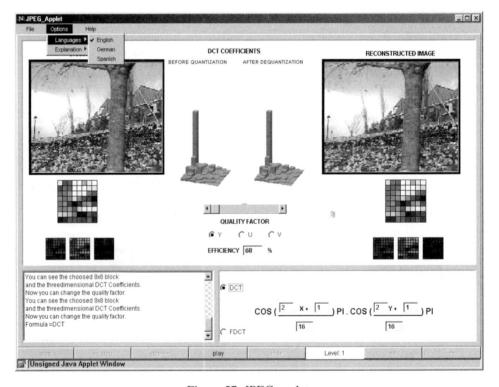

Figure 57: JPEG applet

A.2.2 Preparation unit

In order to understand how an image is prepared to be processed by a compression algorithm, we developed an applet that shows how this preparation is done. In this sense the user will explore that this act is a slightly lossy one. He can choose the number of pixel a block should be.

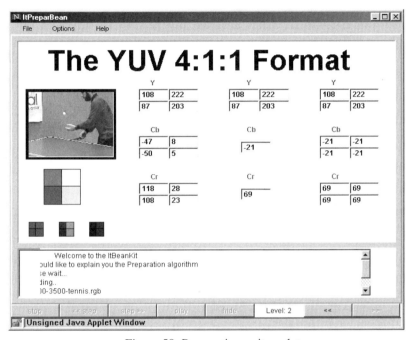

Figure 58: Preparation unit applet

For color images, Red-Green-Blue (RGB) values are transformed into a luminance/chrominance color space (YC_bC_r, YUV, etc.). The luminance component is greyscale and the other two axes are color information. The reason for doing this is that one can afford to lose a lot more information in the chrominance components than in the luminance component: the human eye is not as sensitive to high-frequency chrome information as it is to high-frequency luminance. Usually it is not necessary to change the color space, since the remainder of the algorithm works on each color component independently, and doesn't care just what the data is. However, compression will be less since all components have to be coded at luminance quality. Note that color space transformation is slightly lossy due to round off errors, but the amount of errors is much smaller than what we typically introduce later on. The user down-samples each component by averaging together groups of pixels. The luminance component is left at full resolution, while the chrome components are often reduced 2:1 horizontally and either 2:1 or 1:1 (no change) vertically. In JPEG these alternatives are usually called 2h2v and 2h1v sampling, but one may also see the terms "411" and "422" sampling. This step immediately reduces the data volume by one-half or one-third. In numerical terms it is highly lossy, but for most images it has almost no impact on perceived quality, because of the eye's poorer resolution for chrome information. Note that down-sampling is not applicable to greyscale data; this is one reason why color images are more compressible than greyscale.

A.2.3 Discrete Cosine Transformation (DCT)

The DCT is a relative of the Fourier transform and likewise gives a frequency map, with 8x8 pixel-blocks. Thus numbers are representing the average value in each block and successively higher-frequency changes within the block. The motivation for doing this is that high-frequency information can now be thrown away without affecting low-frequency information. The DCT transform itself is reversible except for round off errors. In each block, each of the 64 frequency components is divided by a separate "humanisation coefficient", and the results are rounded to integers. This is the fundamental information-losing step. The larger the quantization coefficients, the more data is discarded. Note that even the minimum possible quantization coefficient, 1, loses some information, because the exact DCT outputs are typically not integers. Higher frequencies are always quantized less accurately (given larger coefficients) than lower, since they are less visible to the eye.

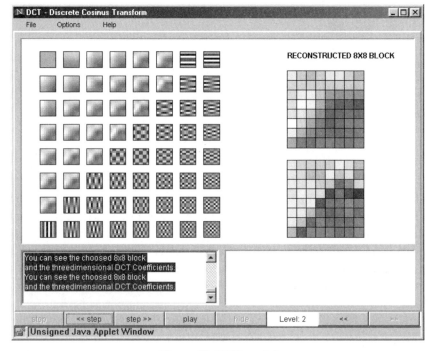

Figure 59: DCT applet

A.2.4 Huffman and Runlength Coding

The reduced coefficients can be encoded using either Huffman, runlength or arithmetic coding. The user will notice that this step is lossless, so it doesn't affect image quality. Because of the nature of these encoding algorithm, these applets are developed to use both data images and text as input.

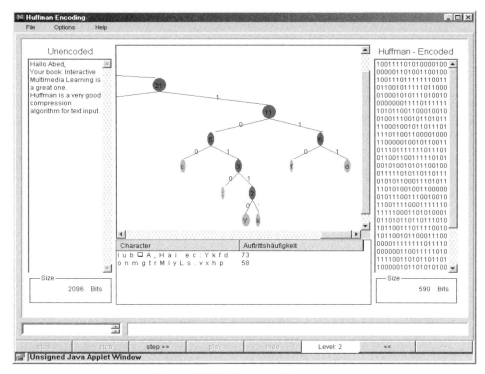

Figure 60: Huffmann coding applet

Appendix B. LOM

B.1 Basic Structure

The definition of LOM divides the descriptors of a learning object in meaningful categories. The actual version of this standard proposal (v. 5) issued on November 11. 2000, introduces 9 such categories [LOM]:

- **General** groups all context-independent features plus the semantic descriptors for the resource.
- **Lifecycle** groups the features linked to the lifecycle of the resource.
- **MetaMetadata** groups the features of the description itself (rather than those of the resource being described.
- **Technical** groups the technical features of the resource.
- **Educational** groups the educational and pedagogic features of the resource.
- **Rights** groups the features that deal with the conditions of use for the resource.
- **Relation** groups features of the resource that link it to other resources.
- **Annotation** allows for comments on the educational use of the resource.
- **Classification** deals with characteristics of the resource described by entries in classifications.

Taken all together, these categories form what is called the Base Scheme.. All of categories and elements are defined as optional. The following diagram illustrates the structure of LOM Base. Each category and it's elements will be introduced in detail later in this chapter.

B.1.1 Data Elements

Categories contain data elements. For each element, the base scheme defines:

- name: how the meta-data element is called
- explanation: the definition of the element
- multiplicity: how many elements are allowed and whether their order is significant
- domain: constraints on appropriate values for the data element
- type: whether the element's value is textual, a date or a reserved element
- note: additional explanations, guidelines for using the element, etc.

B.1.2 List Values

In some instances, a data element can contain a list of values, rather than a single value. This list can be:

- **ordered:** This means that the order of the values in the list is important. A typical example is the list of authors of a publication: the first author is often considered the more important one.
- **unordered:** In an unordered list, the order of the values bears no meaning. As an example, if the description of a simulation includes a short text that describes the intended educational use in three different human languages (for instance: French, German and Italian), then neither of these texts is 'first', or 'prior to the other ones'.

B.1.3 Vocabularies

For some data elements, vocabularies are defined: these are lists of appropriate values. Vocabularies can be:

- **restricted:** This means that only the values from the list specified in this document are acceptable.
- **best practice:** In that case, a list of suggested best practice values is provided, but other values are also acceptable.

B.1.4 Multiplicity

For those elements that have subelements, multiplicity in the Base Scheme applies to tuples of those subelements. As an example, the multiplicity of General.CatalogEntry applies to tuples that contain values for the subelements Catalogue and Entry. In other words, the Base Scheme defines that the value of the element CatalogEntry is an unordered list of (Catalogue,Entry) elements.

B.1.5 Minmax Values

In the base scheme, minmax values are defined for:

- Elements with a list value: Any application is supposed to support at least that number of entries for the list. In other words: an application can impose a maximum on the number of entries it supports for the list value of that element, but that maximum cannot be lower than the minmax value.
- Elements with type String or LangStringType: Any application is supposed to support at least that length for the String value (either directly or contained in the LangStringType) of that element. In other words: an application can impose a maximum on the number of characters it supports for the string value of that element, but that maximum cannot be lower than the minmax value for the type of the element.

B.1.6 Character Sets

The LOM specification defines a conceptual structure for learning object metadata. It does not deal with representation issues, which will be dealt with in separate specifications. Whatever decisions are made in documents that deal with representation, it is a firm expectation by the contributors of the LOM document that such decisions will be taken with a view to support multiple languages. This will have important repercussions with respect to the character sets to be supported.

B.1.7 Derived Schemes

The metadata structure defined in this document is called the Base Scheme. From the Base Scheme, other schemes can be derived. Derived schemes inherit the structure from which they are derived. A derived scheme can add additional categories and data elements, but only to describe characteristics not taken into account in the Base Scheme. A common Base Scheme provides a high degree of interoperability and ("genetic") similarity among different derived schemes.

It is important to note that the properties described by optional data elements can only be described through these optional elements and no overlapping data elements can be introduced.

A particular derived scheme may be more restrictive. For instance, a derived scheme can define some elements as mandatory that are optional or conditional in the Base Scheme. But a derived scheme cannot be less restrictive.

B.1.8 Indexation

Not all values for data elements need to be specified manually by each individual indexer or searcher. In many cases, the values could come from automated processes or templates that specify what is common for a number of objects. This implies that a user describing objects, or someone searching for appropriate material, would only be confronted with a subset of the elements in the Base Scheme.

B.1.9 Representation

For each of the data elements, the specification includes the data type it derives its values from, like LangStringType, DateType, etc. These will be defined separately, and will be implemented in a particular way in a particular system. In order to maximize interoperability, future work may define a common representation for these data types. In the absence of such a common representation, an exchange format (like for instance XML) would allow systems with different representations to still achieve interoperability through a conversion process.

B.1.10 Conformance

A metadata instance conforms to LOM if it satisfies the following four requirements:

- The metadata instance must contain one or more LOM element(s).
- All LOM elements in the metadata instance are used to describe characteristics as defined by the LOM specification. (For example, this means that one shall not abuse the title element to describe the fonts used in the document.)
- Values for LOM elements in the metadata instance are structured as defined by the LOM specification and this structural information is carried within the instance (This means

that the grouping in categories and subelements needs to be maintained. But it does not mean that representations cannot define mappings of this structure as they see fit. More specifically, an XML representation can use the lang attribute to represent the Language element of a LangStringType value.) or Bindings must carry equivalent information about the metadata so that conversions between bindings do not induce loss of information as defined within the specification.

- If the instance contains extensions to the LOM structure, then extension elements do not replace elements in the LOM structure.

A metadata application conforms to LOM if it satisfies the following two requirements:

- A LOM conforming application must be able to process at least one LOM element. If an application receives a conforming LOM metadata instance, stores it, and then transmits it, then the application preserves the original metadata instance during retransmission. If part of the metadata instance is changed, then a new metadata instance is created.
- The application is not required to preserve elements beyond the min-max items of a list or the characters beyond the min-max of a string. Preservation means that the original instance is not changed in any way. i.e. that it "doesn't change a comma".

B.2 LOM Categories

Category	Explanation	Data Type
General	Basic reference to the resource	
l--Identifier	A unique label for the resource	Identifier
l--Title	Name given to the resource	LangString
l--Catalog Entry	Designation given to the resource	SourceString
Characteristics	Non-contextualized features of the resource	
l--Language	The human language of the intellectual content or the application interface	Locale
l--Description	A textual description of the content of the resource	LangString
l--Discipline	A specific knowledge domain	-
l--l--TaxonPath	A taxonomic path in a specific taxonomy.	-
l--l--l--Source	A specific taxonomy	Source

Table 16: LOM Categories

Category	Explanation	Data Type
|--|--|--Taxon	An entry from a taxonomy that refers to the discipline	Entry
|--|--Description	A textual description of the discipline	LangString
|--|--Keywords	Keywords describing the discipline	LangString
|--Coverage	The spatial or temporal characteristics of the intellectual content of the resource	Coverage
|--Concepts	The idea or notion presented in the resource	E.g. invariance, evolutionary, proof, taxonomy
|--Type	The kind of resource	E.g. hypertext, video clip, exercise, simulation, questionnaire
|--Approach	Logical structure used in the resource	Inductive, deductive
|--Granularity	The relative size of the resource	Curriculum, course, unit, topic, lesson, fragment
|--Structure	Underlying organizational structure of the resource	E.g. linear, hyperdimensional, branched, parcelled, atomic, poly
|--Interaction quality	Level of interactivity between an end user and the resource	E.g. low, medium, high
|--Semantic density	Relationship between the usage time and the amount of content presented in the resource	E.g. low, medium, high
Life Cycle	Characteristics related to the different phases of the resource	
|--Version	The edition of the resource	Decimal
|--Status	The condition the resource is in	E.g. draft, final, revised
|--Create	Origin and edition of the resource	-
|--|--Date	The date the resource was created or edited	Date

Table 16: LOM Categories

Category	Explanation	Data Type
I--I--Contribute	Involvement in the creation or edition or the resource	-
I--I--I--Role	Kind of involvement	Vocabulary
I--I--I--Person	Person involved	Person
I--Publish	Making the resource available	-
I--I--Organization	A university, department, company, agency, institute, etc. under whose responsibility the resource was published	Organization
I--I--Date	The date the resource was published	Date
I--Terminate	Making the resource no longer available	-
I--I--Date	The date on which the resource ceases to be accessible	Date
I--Initiated by	Requesting that the resource be produced	-
I--I--I--Person	Person initiating the production of the resource	Person
I--I--Organization	Organization initiating the production of the resource	Organization
Meta-metadata	Characteristics of the description rather than the resource	
I--Create	Origin and edition of the metadata	-
I--I--Date	The date the description was created or edited	Date
I--I--Person	Person that created the description	Person
I--I--Organization	A university, department, company, agency, institute, etc. under whose responsibility the description was published	Organization
I--Scheme	Defines the structure of the metadata. This includes version	E.g. Base 1.0, IMS, ARIADNE
I--Validate	Verification of the quality of the description by a third, authorised party	-
I--I--Date	The date that the description was validated	Date

Table 16: LOM Categories

Category	Explanation	Data Type
|--|--Person	Person that validated the description	Person
|--|--Organization	A university, department, company, agency, institute, etc. under whose responsibility the description was validated	Organization
Technical	Technical features of the resource	
|--Format	Technical data type of the resource	Format
|--Size	The actual size of the digital resource in bytes	Integer
|--LocSpec	A location or a method that resolves to a location	LocSpec
|--OSRequirements	Needs with respect to the Operating System in order to access the resource	-
|--|--OperatingSystem	Name of the Operating System	E.g. MacOS, Unix, Windows95, Windows NT, Generic
|--|--MinimumVersion	Lowest version number of the Operating System	Decimal
|--|--MaximumVersion	Highest version of the Operating System	Decimal
|--OtherPlatformRequirements	Information about other software and hardware requirements	LangString
|--InstallationRemarks	Description on how to install the resource	LangString
|--Duration	Time a continuos resource takes	TimeSpan
Educational Use Dependent	Features that need to be interpreted according to the educational use of the resource	

Table 16: LOM Categories

Category	Explanation	Data Type
I--Role	Kind of use of the resource	E.g. teacher, learner, author, co-ordinator
I--Description	Comment on how the resource is to be used	LangString
I--Prerequisite	Course and/or capabilities required from the end user	-
I--I--Description	Verbal description of the prerequisite	LangString
I--I--Source	Source of the description	Source
I--I--Identifier	Unique identifier of an educational objective within the Source of the Prerequisite	Identifier
I--Educational objective	Intended learning result	-
I--I--Description	Verbal description of the educational objective	LangString
I--I--Source	Source of the description	Source
I--I--Identifier	Unique identifier of an educational objective within the Source of the Prerequisite	Identifier
I--Level	Target audience	Vocabulary
I--Difficulty	How hard it is to work through the resource	E.g. low, medium, high
I--Duration	Time it takes to work with the resource	TimeSpan
Rights Management	Features that need to be interpreted according to the use of the resource	
I--Role	Kind of use of the resource	E.g. read, incorporate, resell
I--Description	Comment on the use of the resource	LangString
I--Contact	A steward that can assist with rights procurement	LocSpec
I--Support	Whether or not support is available for the resource	Boolean
I--Conditions	Legal or economic requirements for use according to the role	-

Table 16: LOM Categories

Category	Explanation	Data Type
|--|--Reciprocity	Whether or not the provider of a resource can use any resource that incorporates his resource on the same basis	Boolean
|--|--Attribution	Whether or not the use of a resource requires it be cited	Boolean
|--|--Price	Amount of money to be paid to use the resource in the way specified by role	-
|--|--|--Monetary Unit	Unit of currency referred to by Amount	E.g. BEF, US$, FrFr
|--|--|--Amount	Monetary value	Decimal
|--|--|--Unit of pricing	Unit of which the price applies	E.g. flat fee, per hour, per MByte
Relation	Characteristics of the resource in relationship to other resources	
|--Kind	Nature of the relationship between the resources	E.g. IsPartOf, HasPart, IsVersionOf, HasVersion, IsFormatOf, HasFormat, References, IsReferencedBy, IsBasedOn, IsBasisFor, Requires, IsRequiredBy
|--Resource	Resource the relationship holds for	-
|--|--Identifier	Unique Identifier of the other resource	Identifier
IEEE Name	Explanation	Data Type
|--|--Description	Description of the other resource	LangString
Annotation	Comments on the use of the resource	
|--Person	Annotator	Person
|--Date	Date that the annotation was created	Date
|--Description	The content of the annotation	LangString

Table 16: LOM Categories

Appendix C. On-line-Questionnaire

You are on the questionnaire web page of Multibook. To answer the questions properly you need to work through the parade lesson "Ethernet". You have to watch both the visualizations accompanied by the explanation of the lesson as well as the interactive simulation at the end of the lesson. The lesson on "Ethernet" can be found on the web by clicking on the following link:

http://www.kom.e-technik.tu-darmstadt.de/projects/iteach/itbeankit/html/.

You can start answering the questions after working through the lesson and understanding the concepts behind Ethernet.

Some of the questions address the lesson as a unit. They address hypermedia learning in general and try to gain insight whether hypermedia learning environment, enhanced with multimedia elements, help learners to understand the topics better. Other questions address the use of the same visualization in different context. Finally, some questions deal with the interactive simulation at the end of the lesson.

With visualization we mean applets which are embedded in the lesson, and where the degree of interactivity is low, while with simulation we mean the applet at the end of the lesson, where the Ethernet protocol is simulated and where users can highly interact with the applet and build their own scenarios.

C.1 Questions

Questions concerning the way users had worked with the system:

- How many of the visualizations did you work with?
  (all, most of them, almost half of them, few of them, none)
- How often did you look at a visualization addressing a specific question or topic?
  (several times, once, I did not work with a visualization till the end, none)
- How intensive did you work with the simulation?
  (In level 3 I defined my own scenario; I tried it till level 2; I worked only with level 1; I did not work with the simulation)

Please specify which of the following predications apply:
(fully apply, well apply, partly apply, does not apply at all)

- I enjoyed working with the visualizations.
- I enjoyed working with the simulation.
- The similarity of the visualizations is monotonous and tedious.
- The visualizations helped me to better understand the functionality of Ethernet.
- The visualizations were not really necessary to better understand the functionality of Ethernet.
- The contemplation of the visualizations cost me unnecessarily time.
- The simulation helped me to better understand the functionality of Ethernet.
- The simulation at the end of the lesson was not really necessary to better understand the functionality of Ethernet
- It would have been better to have the simulation at the beginning of the lesson instead of having it at the end.

Questions concerning the suitability of interactive multimedia learning units in diverse learn situations and activities:

- In which of the following learning situations would you like to use instructional visualization embedded in hypermedia learn environment? (more than one answer is possible)
  - Self study (no need to the lecturer)
  - Preparation and/or post processing of the lecture
  - Preparation of the exams
  - As a general knowledge source
  - No utilization at all
- In which of the following learning activities would you like to use instructional visualization embedded in hypermedia learn environment? (more than one answer is possible)
  - First acquisition of knowledge
  - Deepening of knowledge
  - Repeating and freshening of knowledge
  - Well directed acquisition of information
  - Procuring an overview
  - No utilization at all

Questions concerning technical and usability problems and/or difficulties:

- Did you have any technical problems?
  (yes, no, which: _____)
- Did you have any difficulties to navigate through the lesson?
  (yes, no, which: _____)
- Did you have any difficulties to interact with the visualizations?
  (yes, no, which: _____)
- Did you have any difficulties to interact with the simulation?
  (yes, no, which: _____)

Appendix D. List of Developed Visualizations

As a part of the Multibook project we developed several instructional visualizations. These modules have been implemented as Java applets that illustrate concepts and algorithms of multimedia communication technology. We use these components for the multimedia communication courses being taught at Darmstadt University of Technology. They are built as units with a broad focus, illustrating many different sub-topics of the concept they were designed to visualize and teach for, allowing students to experiment with many different combinations of parameters.

An actual list of all applets can be found at:

*   http://www.kom.e-technik.tu-darmstadt.de/Teaching/Visualization/visualization.html
*   http://www.kom.e-technik.tu-darmstadt.de/projects/iteach/itbeankit/html/
*   http://www.multibook.de/Animationen/animationen.html

Some of these applets are also included in the Multibook CD published by Springer-Verlag [Ste00]

D.1 Complete Lessons

*   Parade lesson: Ethernet
*   Parade lesson: Diskscheduling
*   Parade lesson: JPEG

D.2 Stand-alone Applets

D.2.1 Animations

*   VRML (Virtual Reality Modeling Language)

D.2.2 Disk Scheduling Algorithms

*   FCFS (First Come First Served)
*   SCAN
*   C_SCAN
*   EDF (Earliest Deadline First)
*   SCAN-EDF
*   Accurate-Scan-EDF
*   Group Sweeping
*   Compare all algorithm
*   compare each alg. with himself and or with other alg.

D.2.3 Compression

- JPEG
- Preparation unit
- Discrete Cosine Transformation (DCT)
- Inverse Discrete Cosine Transformation (IDCT)
- Run-Length encoding
- Run-Length decoding
- Huffman encoding
- Huffman decoding
- Huffman encoding/decoding

D.2.4 Multimedia Communications

- HTTP (HyperText Transfer Protocol)
- TCP (Transmission Control Protocol)
- Sliding Window
- Mobile IP
- Ethernet
- Switch
- HUB

And now for something completely different.
— Monthy Python's Flying Circus

Index

Dynamic metadata 55
Static metadata 55
Model-View-Controller (MVC) 32, 81, 122
Controller 33
Model 33
View 33
Movie and Stills 21
MPEG 41
Multibook 59, 61, 67, 68, 76, 79, 102
Multilingual information access 84

N

NetMeeting 103, 107, 110, 123
Non-systematic reuse 31

O

Object Oriented Frameworks 34
Object-Oriented Programming (OOP)29, 48
Ontology 65
OpenDoc 47

P

Parametrization of interactive
visualizations 57
Polymorphism 30
Properties 43

R

Read-only property 43
Real-time 111, 124
Red-Green-Blue 163
Reliable communication 102
Reliable multicast 112
Rendering delay 129, 130
Replicated architecture 105
Resource Description Framework (RDF)49
Reusability measuremen 90
Reusability of content 27

S

Server Processing Delay 125, 127
SFK   65

SharedX 103, 106, 110, 123
Smalltalk Frame Kit 65
Software architecture 32
Software metrics 90
Software reuse in learning systems 28
Sorting out Sorting 17
SQL database 73
Synchronous tools 101

T

TANGO 19
TCP   102, 112, 124

U

UDP   102, 112
UML   40, 56, 116

V

VCR   82, 83, 88
Visual programming 11
VisualBasic 40
Visualization 8, 56, 58, 61, 69, 87, 91, 94,
101, 121
Algorithm 11
Computation 10
Engineering 9
Information 10
Mathematical 10
Program 10
Scientific 9

W

Warwick Framework 49
Write-only property 43

X

XML 76
xTango19

Z

Zeus   18